Series / Number 01-040

The Politics of
Economic Policy in the   U.S.
United States:
A Tentative View from a
Comparative Perspective

ANDREW MARTIN
Boston University

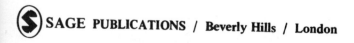

SAGE PUBLICATIONS / Beverly Hills / London

For information address:

SAGE PUBLICATIONS, INC.
275 South Beverly Drive
Beverly Hills, California 90212

SAGE PUBLICATIONS, INC.
St George's House / 44 Hatton Garden
London EC1N 8ER

International Standard Book Number 0-8039-0254-9

Library of Congress Catalog Card No. L.C. 73-80266

FIRST PRINTING

When citing a professional paper, please use the proper form. Remember to cite the
correct Sage Professional Paper series title and include the paper number. One of the
two following formats can be adapted (depending on the style manual used):

(1) NAMENWIRTH, J. Z. and H. D. LASSWELL (1970) The Changing Language of
American Values: A Computer Study of Selected Party Platforms. Sage
Professional Paper in Comparative Politics 01-001. Beverly Hills and London:
Sage Pubns.

OR

(2) Namenwirth, J. Zvi and Harold D. Lasswell, *The Changing Language of American
Values: A Computer Study of Selected Party Platforms.* Beverly Hills and
London: Sage Professional Paper in Comparative Politics 01-001, 1970.

CONTENTS

The Politics of Economic Policy in the United States: A Tentative View from a Comparative Perspective

ANDREW MARTIN
Boston University

I. INTRODUCTION

The purpose of this paper is to suggest some ways in which comparative analysis might help to identify and explain the distinctive features of the pattern of economic policy pursued in the United States. It proceeds in essentially two stages. The first describes variations in certain significant dimensions of economic policy within a group of countries, including the United States, that can be said to have the same basic type of political economy. In this way, an attempt is made to define what it is that is to be explained. The second stage explores variations in certain features of the political systems in the countries concerned that seem to have a bearing on the observed variations in the patterns of economic policy. In this way, an attempt is made to identify the political factors that may help to explain the policy variations.

Without elaborating a general typology of political economies, we can define the political economy common to the group of countries in which the United States is included simply in terms of certain obvious characteristics of the institutions that organize political and economic

AUTHOR'S NOTE: *This paper was presented at the 1972 Annual Meeting of the American Political Science Association. It was written while the author was a Research Fellow in the West European Studies Program and Center for International Affairs at Harvard University, whose support and stimulation he hereby gratefully acknowledges.*

processes in these countries. On the one hand, control of governmental authority in these countries depends on the outcome of recurrent elections in which there are freely competing candidates, grouped however tightly or loosely in separate political formations. On the other hand, most production of goods and services is organized within the framework of private property institutions and directed to markets in which there are varying degrees of competition among autonomous units. Accordingly, and in the absence of any better terminology, we will adopt the term, "plural party capitalist"[1] to refer to political economies with these characteristics. The group with which we are concerned can be further delimited by confining it to plural party capitalist political economies in advanced industrial societies—that is, societies in which the vast majority of the labor force is in nonagricultural occupations and white-collar workers soon will or already account for a larger proportion of the total than blue-collar workers.

To define the group in this way is to include in it the countries scattered from North America, through most of Western Europe, to Japan, Australia, and New Zealand. In effect, the definition simply embodies the assumption that, for our purposes at least, it can be illuminating to compare the politics of economic policy in these countries. Given the similarities in the institutions that organize political and economic processes, the patterns of interaction among actors with various roles in those institutions are also similar in the countries concerned. The interactions are structured, within and between political arenas and markets, in familiar ways—e.g., firms, labor unions, peak associations, political parties, and so forth. These interactions, in turn, are associated with common tendencies in the roles of governments within these political economies, manifested in common characteristics of the patterns of economic policy pursued by governments in all of the countries in the group. It is the variations within these common patterns of policy with which this discussion is concerned.

Specifically, the discussion is focused on variations in what would seem to be two important and closely related economic roles that governments typically perform in the plural party capitalist group. One is the use of fiscal and monetary instruments to manage aggregate demand in such a way as to keep unemployment at low levels, relative to those between the two world wars—that is, to maintain full employment, at whatever level it may be defined. The other is to use a variety of fiscal instruments to channel funds through the public sector in ways that provide supplements or alternatives to income from employment or other sources, and that provide for the collective supply of services and goods such as education, health, and housing. To the extent that governments use these instruments in these ways, they can be said to approximate a "full employment welfare state" pattern of policy.[2]

This is admittedly a rather awkward expression, but it calls attention to elements of policy whose interdependence should probably be recognized as a fundamental feature of the patterns of policy pursued within the plural party capitalist group since the end of the second world war, and already before the war in one or more cases.[3] It is true that the welfare state elements have histories that go considerably farther back in time. Yet, the great Depression seems to have made it clear that they were not sustainable until the strategies for managing aggregate demand identified with the Keynesian Revolution were established, and this has been largely a postwar phenomenon. Thus, for example, the interdependence of the two elements was an explicit premise underlying Sir William Beveridge's famous program for postwar reconstruction in Britain, and it would seem to be a fundamentally valid premise (Beveridge, 1944: 11, 17-18; Social Insurance and Allied Services, 1942: 163-165).

The particular mix of policies implemented in early postwar Britain was, of course, only one variant of the pattern with which we are concerned. In Britain and elsewhere there have been developments in the theory and practice of economic policy that may be described as post-Beveridgean as well as post-Keynesian, and also developments that are in some respects alternatives to the specific variants envisioned by Keynes and Beveridge. Not all of the developments can be said to go "beyond the welfare state" in any of its variants, however. Some amount to retreats from the full employment welfare state to higher levels of unemployment, restriction of the scope of public sector welfare state institutions relative to private sector counterparts (but not equivalents), and the return to punitive "poor law" approaches in the public sector.[4] These diverse developments have generated some of the central issues in the politics of economic policy in plural party capitalist countries. Conflict over such issues has at times reached an intensity that was apparently unexpected in the early postwar years when it seemed to some that the issues were largely settled, accompanied by an "end of ideology."[5] Thus, the changes in the degree to which the full employment welfare state pattern is approximated in any country are by no means always in the direction of a fuller approximation. A systematic analysis of the dynamics of political conflict over these dimensions of economic policy would seem well worth making, but it lies beyond the scope of this paper. Perhaps the paper can nevertheless at least suggest some of the lines along which such an analysis might proceed.

While the discussion that follows is set within a comparative framework that embraces all the countries in the plural party capitalist group in principle, it falls far short of that in practice. Particular attention is concentrated on the United States and, to a lesser extent, on Sweden. Part II of the paper presents a survey of the variations in some dimensions of the full employment welfare state pattern of policy among the countries for which comparable data were readily available. On the basis of the survey, it is suggested that the United States and Sweden are at or near the opposite ends of the range of variation in many dimensions of this pattern of policy. Part III discusses some of the characteristics of the American political system, drawing on some ideas advanced by a number of writers on the subject. On the basis of these ideas, a hypothesis is proposed that seems to relate some of the distinctive features of the American polity to the distinctive pattern of policy in the United States suggested by the survey in Part II. In Part IV, the hypothesis is elaborated further in the light of some European cases. Finally, in Part V, the way in which the hypothesis might explain the distinctive pattern of policy discerned in the United States is illustrated by a discussion of a major recent fiscal policy decision that was consistent with that pattern, the Kennedy-Johnson tax-cut of 1963-1964.

II. VARIATIONS IN THE PATTERN OF POLICY

UNEMPLOYMENT

It has repeatedly been noted that unemployment levels in the United States have tended to be substantially higher than in Western Europe during the postwar period. As is also well known, it is difficult to determine just how much higher unemployment has been in the United States because unemployment data from various countries are not entirely comparable for a variety of reasons. However, reasonably careful efforts to adjust foreign unemployment figures to make them approximately comparable with American data have been made by the U.S. Department of Labor. In a recent report, it compared unemployment here with adjusted estimates of unemployment in seven other countries during the sixties—Canada, France, Britain, Sweden, Italy, West Germany, and Japan (Sorrentino, 1970). These are, of course, the major countries in the group with which we are concerned.

On the basis of these figures, the United States and Sweden lie toward but not at the opposite ends of the range of variation in levels of unemployment among the eight countries (see Table 1). However, the only country in which average unemployment during the decade was higher than in the United States was Canada, the country whose economy is most closely integrated with the United States economy. Canada's average unemployment between 1960 and 1969 was 5.1%, while the United States average over the same decade was 4.8%. The United States average was close to three times higher than the Swedish average, which was 1.7%. Two of the other countries had even lower averages than Sweden, however. West Germany's average of 0.6% was the lowest and Japan's 1.3% second lowest. The other three countries had unemployment levels lying between those in the high level North American pair and the three low level countries. Of the three in the middle group, France had the lowest with 2.3%, Britain was next with 2.8%, and Italy was considerably higher with 3.7%. Italy's level, more than a percentage point lower than that in the United States, would undoubtedly have been closer to the U.S. level if it had not been for the substantial emigration to other European countries with high demand for labor, especially West Germany (Sorrentino, 1970: 14-15).

Comparable data for all of these countries during the fifties have not been made available. However, we can extend the comparison of unemployment in the United States and Sweden back over that decade by adjusting the available Swedish data to make them at least roughly

TABLE 1
UNEMPLOYMENT RATES IN EIGHT COUNTRIES, 1960-1969[a]

Year	United States	Canada	France	Great Britain	Italy	Japan	Sweden	West Germany
1960	5.5	7.0	2.5	2.0	4.3	1.7	1.6[b]	0.8
1961	6.7	7.1	1.9	1.9	3.7	1.5	1.5	0.5
1962	5.5	5.9	1.8	2.8	3.2	1.3	1.5	0.4
1963	5.7	5.5	2.1	3.5	2.7	1.3	1.7	0.5
1964	5.2	4.7	1.6	2.5	3.0	1.2	1.5	0.3
1965	4.5	3.9	2.0	2.2	4.0	1.2	1.2	0.3
1966	3.8	3.6	2.1	2.4	4.3	1.4	1.6	0.3
1967	3.8	4.1	2.7	3.8	3.8	1.3	2.1	1.0
1968	3.6	4.8	3.2	3.7	3.8	1.2	2.2	1.2
1969	3.5	4.7	2.8	3.7	3.7	1.1	1.9	0.7
Average	4.8	5.1	2.3	2.8	3.7	1.3	1.7	0.6

SOURCE: Sorrentino (1970: 14).
a. Data for countries other than the United States and Canada adjusted to United States concepts.
b. Not available in source. Rate for 1960 is from insured unemployment series in Lindbeck (1968: 206), linked to series in source in 1961.

comparable with the Department of Labor's series (see Table 2). On this basis, the difference between the average levels of unemployment in the two countries appears to have been only slightly less in the fifties than the sixties. It was 4.5% in the United States and 1.9% in Sweden during the earlier decade, compared with 4.8% and 1.7%, respectively, in the later one. In contrast with the sixties, though, the U.S. level was slightly higher than the level in Canada, for which published data are essentially comparable (Smith, 1966: 18). I have not tried to adjust fifties data for the other countries to the Department of Labor's series for the sixties. But on the basis of trends discernible in the published data and various other adjusted series, it is evident that unemployment in the United States was higher than in Western Europe during the first of the two decades as well as the second (Gordon, 1967: 8; Maddison, 1964: 220). The major difference in the relative positions of the various countries was in the case of West Germany, which started the fifties with what was clearly the highest levels of unemployment, dropping sharply as immigration from the East was absorbed and then ceased altogether (Edelman and Fleming, 1965: 109; Ulman and Flanagan, 1971: 174).

UNEMPLOYMENT VERSUS INFLATION

While the level of unemployment in the United States has tended to be higher than in Sweden and in the other countries in the group outside North America, the rate at which prices have increased in the United States has tended to be lower than in the other countries in the group, as all the literature on Phillips curves would lead us to expect. When the relationships between unemployment levels and price increase rates in the United States and Sweden are compared over the fifties and sixties, the contrast that emerges is striking (see Table 2). In the United States, the average annual level of unemployment was 2.2 and 2.1 times higher than the average annual percentage increase of the consumer price index during the fifties and sixties, respectively. In Sweden, the average annual level of unemployment was a little over a half and a little less than half of the average annual percentage increases in the consumer price index in the corresponding periods. To put it the other way around, in Sweden, the average rates of price increases were 1.9 and 2.2 times the average levels of unemployment in the two decades, while in the United States the corresponding ratios were about 0.5 and 0.5.

I have not attempted to calculate comparable ratios for the other countries but the price data consulted for most of them show higher rates of price increases in them than in the United States over the two-decade period (Smith, 1966: 14). Thus, while it has not been ascertained that

TABLE 2
UNEMPLOYMENT AND INFLATION IN THE UNITED STATES AND SWEDEN, 1950-1969

	United States	Sweden
	%	%
Average unemployment		
1950-1959	4.5[a]	1.9[b]
1960-1969	4.8[a]	1.7[b]
Average increase in consumer prices		
1950-1959	2.1[c]	3.4[d]
1960-1969	2.3[c]	3.8[e]
Ratio of unemployment to price increases		
1950-1959	2.2	0.54
1960-1969	2.1	0.45
Ratio of price increases to unemployment		
1950-1959	0.45	1.9
1960-1969	0.49	2.2

a. Economic Report of the President (1971: 222).
b. The insured unemployment rate for 1950-1961 (Lindbeck, 1968: 206) was adjusted by the ratio of the 1961 rate in this series to the 1961 unemployment rate in the series for Sweden, 1961-1969, adjusted to U.S. concepts by Sorrentino (1970: 14), based on Swedish sample survey data beginning in 1961.
c. Average of annual percentage changes in the consumer price index (Economic Report of the President, 1971: 249).
d. Average of annual percentage increases in the consumer price index (Statistisk årsbok, 1968: 216).
e. Average of annual percentage increases in the consumer price index (The Swedish Economy, 1970, 1: Table 32; 1972, 2: Table 32).

Sweden is at the end of the range of variation in the observed tradeoff between unemployment and inflation at which the ratio of price increases to unemployment is greatest, it seems pretty clear that the United States is at the opposite end at which the ratio of unemployment to price increases is greatest.

Since the level of price increases associated with a given level of unemployment differs from country to country and over time, depending on all the economic factors that enter into each country's Phillips curve or whatever the relationship may be, one cannot draw any unambiguous political conclusions from the observable ratios between price increases and unemployment. The data cited nevertheless convey a familiar picture. As R. A. Gordon (1967: 20) sums it up:

> Full employment and rapid growth carry higher priorities in Europe than in the United States. Conversely, price stability has carried a higher priority in the United States.

But whose priorities? At most, apart from the qualification already made, such data can only suggest that those who have shaped economic policy in the United States have put a higher priority on price stability than full employment, and that the priorities of economic policy makers in Sweden and probably the rest of Western Europe have been the reverse. Even this may be to assume too much concerning the relationship between the behavior of the economy and the intentions of economic policy makers. Of course, there is the kind of evidence available that can tell us a good deal more about the differences in the relative weight attached to full employment and price stability by different participants in the process of economic policy formation in various countries—particularly evidence concerning the choices they make at relevant decision points in the process. Gordon drew on evidence of that kind in characterizing the priorities that seem to have dominated economic policy formation in the United States and Western Europe, and a systematic analysis of the evidence would undoubtedly reinforce that characterization.

However, it would hardly be valid to interpret the contrasting relationships between unemployment and price increase that may be established in the United States and Western Europe as reflections of contrasting orders of priority placed on the two goals by "the public" in this country and Europe, as is not infrequently done. To do so is certainly to make extraordinarily naive assumptions about the sources and composition of public opinion, and also about the relationships between the beliefs and expectations that are in fact differentially created and distributed among various publics and the choices made in the policy-making process. In other words, it is to beg the very questions that have to be answered to account for the patterns of policy that come out of that process—such questions as how issues are defined in the various different arenas of conflict over policy, how the capacity for shaping both the definition of issues and the outcome of the conflicts is distributed among the various participants in these arenas, and the like. Before turning to some of the problems involved in trying to find answers to questions such as these, however, it is necessary to sketch in a little more fully the variations in the patterns of economic policy to be accounted for by such answers.

Having suggested the variations in the degree to which full employment is approximated, and to which it is apparently given priority relative to price stability, it is necessary to look at variations in the other component of the full employment-welfare state pattern of policy among the countries in the group with which we are concerned. Viewing it broadly, as suggested earlier, the welfare state component can be said to consist of two general types of policy, those that make a variety of goods and services available and those that transfer income to people. Gauging the degree to which the welfare state in this sense is approximated in different countries necessarily poses more complex problems than those involved in measuring unemployment levels on a comparable basis, problems more complex than we can even begin to deal with within the confines of this paper. We can do no more than point to some data that suggest what the variations might be.

THE PUBLIC SECTOR SHARE OF NATIONAL PRODUCT

Insofar as both types of welfare state policies involve the channeling of funds through the public sector, the public sector share of gross national product can perhaps serve as a first approximation to a single comprehensive indicator, crude as it admittedly is. The Organization for Economic Cooperation and Development's National Accounts Statistics seem to provide a reasonably comparable basis for gauging the public sector share of GNP. Looking at it from the revenue side, which includes all taxes accruing to all levels of government together with those taxes designated as social security "contributions," we once again find a striking contrast between the United States and Sweden, and the rest of Western Europe as well, as we did with respect to unemployment levels (see Figure 1). In revenue terms, the public sector share of GNP (at current market prices) in 1960 was 27% in the United States and 35% in Sweden. By the beginning of the next decade, the public sector share had risen in both countries but much less in the United States than in Sweden. In 1970, it was 31% in the United States, a rise of only four points, while it was 48% in Sweden, a rise of thirteen points. Sweden's 1960 level was just below the West German level of 36%, which was the highest in that year, but the Swedish level soon became the highest and has continued to be the highest in the whole OECD group. (The OECD group includes several countries in addition to those that can be described as plural party capitalist countries). While Sweden has for some years been at the high end of the range of variation in public sector share of GNP within the group with which we are concerned, the United States has been close to, if not quite at, the opposite end of the range. The contrast between the United States and Swedish levels becomes all the more striking in view of the general tendency for the public sector share of GNP to vary with per capita GNP. The United States, with the highest per capita GNP in the OECD group, provides the one major exception to that tendency, leaving Sweden, with the second highest per capita GNP since the mid-sixties, with the highest public sector share. The U.S. public sector share has been at about the

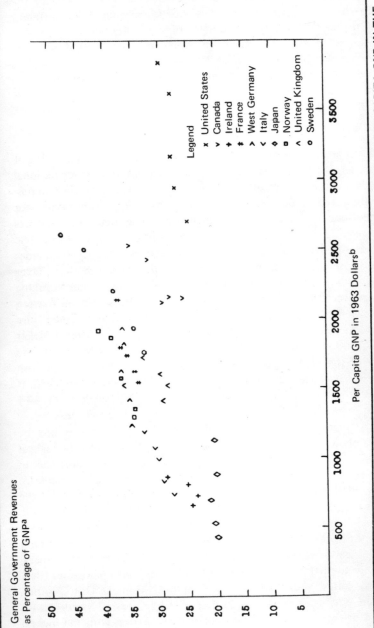

General Government Revenues
as Percentage of GNP[a]

Per Capita GNP in 1963 Dollars[b]

Figure 1: RELATION OF GENERAL GOVERNMENT REVENUES AS A PERCENTAGE OF GNP TO PER CAPITA GNP IN THE UNITED STATES AND NINE OTHER COUNTRIES; 1958, 1960, 1963, 1966 and 1968.

SOURCE: Organization for Economic Co-operation and Development (1970: 10, 13, 342-363).

a. Includes central and local government revenues and social security contributions.

b. Per capita GNP at market prices in U.S. dollars, adjusted by price indices of GNP at market prices, 1963 = 100.

same level as that in Ireland, which ranked lowest in per capita GNP by the end of the sixties after falling behind Japan, which had previously had the lowest per capita GNP in the plural party capitalist group. In other words, while the United States has been the richest country in the group, its public sector share of GNP has been closest to that in one of the poorest countries in the group.

It is, of course, necessary to go far beyond this single indicator, not only looking as well at the expenditure side but also breaking down both revenues and expenditures in such a way as to compare their composition and distributive effects. Again, it is possible to do no more than cite a few illustrative figures. As is to be expected, public sector shares of expenditures, including transfer payments to households, tend to exhibit roughly the same trends as revenues. The United States and Sweden are accordingly at or near the opposite ends of the range of variation in public sector expenditures among the plural party capitalist countries, as indicated by the OECD data (OECD, 1970: 318-363).

The degree to which the welfare state is approximated is presumably somewhat more adequately reflected in the civilian portion of public sector expenditures than in their total. If we therefore deduct military spending from the totals for the United States and Sweden, the difference between them becomes even more marked. In the United States, the nonmilitary public sector share of GNP was 17.8% in 1950, 21.5% in 1960, and 23.7% in 1970 (Economic Report of the President, 1971: 197, 204). In Sweden, it was 21.5% in 1950, 28.4% in 1960, and 38.9% in 1970.[6] Thus, civilian public spending rose in proportion to total output in both countries over the two decades, but much faster in Sweden than the United States.

SOCIAL SECURITY

Obviously, civilian public spending is still too crude a measure, but a systematic disaggregation of the totals to indicate the allocation of resources among the various welfare state functions, depending on different definitions of their scope, would require a much more detailed discussion of specific institutional arrangements than can be provided here. With respect to the range of programs embraced within the broad definition of social security used by the International Labor Organization, a careful statistical analysis by Henry Aaron makes it pretty clear that the United States is at or near the low end of the range of variation among the group of countries in question for us. He summarizes his findings (Aaron, 1967: 44), which refer to a considerably larger group:

Compared to social security in other industrial countries, the United States system is new and modest. It is also relatively narrow. Its limited health insurance system is in its infancy, and it completely eschews family allowances; both are programs which most other countries have adopted. The level of benefits for the aged relative to per capita income is lower in the United States than in most other developed countries. The importance of the age of the system indicated by these regressions, however, suggests that both risks covered and the relative size of benefits will expand as the United States program matures.

Apart from the existence of benefits such as family allowances and comprehensive health insurance in Sweden which do not exist in the United States, perhaps the most illuminating differences between the welfare state institutions lie in the national pension systems that exist on a large scale in both countries. It may be useful to go beyond Aaron's summary at least in this connection. In both countries, the national (i.e., public sector) pension systems provide retirement benefits related to earnings up to certain maxima. Perhaps the best way to compare the benefits provided is to relate the minimum and maximum benefit levels in each country to some measure of the respective average income levels in each. In other words, we can compare the proportion of average earnings replaced by retirement benefits. There are considerable difficulties involved in doing so, however, because of the complexities and the changes going on in the pension systems in both countries, and also because of differences in the income data available for them. While familiarity with the American Old Age, Survivors and Disability Insurance system can presumably be taken for granted, at least a brief discussion of the Swedish system would seem to be a necessary preliminary to such comparisons as can be made.

The Swedish pension system is in the process of transition. Legislation that went into effect in 1960 added a supplementary earnings-related pension scheme to a preexisting system of flat-rate pension benefits (Uhr, 1966: 36-68). The combination of the two types of benefits is designed to provide pensions equivalent to 65% of average earnings during the 15 years of highest earnings, between certain minimum and maximum levels. These lower and upper limits are set in accordance with a base amount that is linked to changes in the consumer price index. The lower limit of pension benefits is the basic flat-rate pension which, during the sixties, was being moved up to a level of 90% of the base amount. The upper limit is determined in relation to a maximum amount of income that can be credited toward supplementary pensions in any year, and that amount is set at seven-and-a-half times the level of the base amount during that year.

The basic flat-rate pension scheme provides a universal minimum income in old age. Thus, all retired couples jointly receive pensions equal to 155% of the basic pension, regardless of their earnings history. On the other hand, the supplementary pensions they receive are dependent entirely on their individual earnings histories. Moreover, to qualify for full supplementary benefits, an individual has to have credited earnings for a minimum number of years, which will increase from 20 to 30 between 1981 and 1991. The year 1981 will be the first in which combined benefits will reach the full level of 65% of the fifteen-year best-earnings average. In other words, the supplementary benefit level is being raised gradually, with the first age cohort with members who will have had qualified earnings for 20 years since the introduction of the scheme retiring in 1981. Those retiring between 1961 and 1981 are treated as a transitional generation, entitled to supplementary pensions according to a formula that sets them at levels that gradually approach the full level to be reached by 1981.

The benefit levels described in these terms only take on meaning when they are related to the actual levels of earnings (see Table 3). Median family income is evidently regarded as the most relevant measure in American discussions of social security (Pechman et al. 1968: 96). As far as I know, the most nearly comparable measure available for Sweden is that for median household income in 1966, provided by a special survey made in early 1967 for a major government study of low income (i.e., poverty).[7] On this basis, the minimum annual pension that every retired couple in Sweden got in 1966 was equivalent to 26% of median household income in that year. At the opposite end of the scale, if both members of a retired couple were eligible for the maximum supplementary benefits available in 1966, their combined basic and supplementary pension would be equivalent to about 77% of median household income. If the supplementary pension scheme had been in full operation in 1966, the high income couple's combined pension would have been equivalent to 216% of median household income. The assumptions underlying this estimated maximum would, of course, apply to a very small proportion of pensioners. Specifically, each of the members of the maximum pension couple would have had to have a fifteen-year average-earning level equivalent to about 186% of median household income during the relevant years.

The point is that the range of benefits built into the Swedish national pension scheme is very wide indeed. Thus, it is designed to include persons with earnings well up in the income hierarchy, not only with respect to benefits that are likely to be attractive to them but also with respect to the base for the payroll tax by which the supplementary portion of the scheme is financed, consequently covering a very large proportion of total earnings.[8] This has a double significance that we shall merely mention here. First, the scheme would appear to be well suited to maintaining a broad constituency for public sector income maintenance institutions by making it difficult for private sector institutions to compete by offering more favorable terms except to a very small proportion of the population. Second, although it would not necessarily have to be if the pension scheme were financed on a pay-as-you-go basis, the payroll tax is in fact set at rates that have resulted in the rapid buildup of a huge fund, with the result that an increasing portion of savings has been channeled through the public sector. The extent to which the national supplementary scheme has in this way preempted the field is indicated by the rapid growth of its accumulated capital compared with the slow growth of the Swedish Personnel Pension Fund, a mutual insurance organization that underwrites most of the separate pension plans set up by private firms. During the period from 1959 to 1968 (for which data for both are available), the National Pension Insurance Fund grew from zero to 26 million crowns, while the SPP Fund grew from 4.8 million to 7.4 million crowns (Statistisk årsbok, 1964: 186; 1970: 199). The National Pension Fund has continued to grow at the same rate, accounting for around 46% of total advances on the Swedish credit market in fiscal year 1970-1971 (The Swedish Economy, 1971, 3: 117). This is in sharp contrast with the growth of private pension plans as a major form of capital accumulation in the United States. Their total reserves grew from $52 billion in 1960 to $125 billion in 1969, over a period in which their benefit outlays only rose from $1.7 billion to $5.9 billion. Essentially a pay-as-you-go system, the U.S. public sector pension system has accumulated a relatively small surplus by comparison with the private pension plans, amounting to only about $30.1 billion in 1969, or about 24% of the private plans' total reserves (U.S. Bureau of the Census, 1971: 283, 285). Obviously, what is at stake in the balance between public and private sector institutions for providing income maintenance in old age is not only the levels and distribution of such income (as well as its reliability and the compatibility of the institutions with labor mobility, and so forth), but also the basic structure of the capital market and control of the funds flowing through it.[9]

As for the pension benefits themselves, it remains to compare those provided by the public sector schemes in Sweden and the United States (see Table 3). According to the 1967 amendments to the Social Security Act, the minimal annual retirement benefit for a couple was equivalent to 12.4% of median family income in 1967, as compared with the Swedish

TABLE 3

RETIREMENT BENEFITS: NATIONAL PENSION SYSTEMS IN THE UNITED STATES, 1967, AND SWEDEN, 1966

	United States	Sweden
Minimum benefit, retired couple	$ 990[a]	7,150[b] Sw.Kr.
Maximum benefit, retired couple	$3,876[a]	17,868[c] Sw.Kr.
		50,050[d] Sw.Kr.
Minimum benefit as percentage of median income[e]	12%	26%
Maximum benefit as percentage of median income[f]	49%	77%
		216%

a. Minimum and maximum benefits for a retired worker, 65 or over, and spouse, in effect in 1968 according to the 1967 amendments to the Social Security Act (Pechman et al., 1968: 320).
b. Basic benefits payable to a retired worker, retiring at the end of 1966 at age 67, and spouse (Board, 1970: 237).
c. Basic and supplementary benefits to a worker retiring at the end of 1966 at age 67, and spouse. Estimated according to provisions applicable to persons with qualifying earnings retiring between the establishment of the supplementary pension scheme and payment of full benefits beginning in 1981, as summarized by Uhr (1966: 60-62) and the applicable base amount of Sw.Kr.5,500 (Statistisk årsbok, 1968: 216).
d. Hypothetical basic plus supplementary benefits estimated according to provisions applicable if full benefits were already payable.
e. Median family income, 1967: $7,974 (U.S. Bureau of the Census, 1970: 324).
f. Median household income, 1966: Sw.Kr.23,410, estimated from data in Svenska folkets inkomster (1970: 215, Table 9:3).

minimum of 26% of median household income in 1966. The corresponding maximum retirement benefit for a U.S. couple was 48.5% of 1967 median family income, compared with the estimated Swedish maximum of 77% in 1966, which will, of course, be higher in each of the successive years until 1981. The difference between the benefit levels in the two countries is certainly marked, even though it has been estimated conservatively to allow for any unnoticed upward bias in the income measures. Moreover, the difference is understated because the 1967 amendments lay down rates for subsequent years in which median family income was higher, so that the benefit levels have actually been lower than those stated at least until the subsequent increase in benefits. In addition, the difference in income maintenance standards for old people in the two countries is probably understated with respect to both coverage and means-tested benefits. The extent to which this may be the case cannot be indicated without a more detailed discussion than can be undertaken here. Nevertheless, the data examined would seem to suffice to establish that there is a substantial difference between the levels of benefits provided by the public sector pension systems in the United States and Sweden. In the absence of a systematic comparison of such benefits on the same basis for all the plural party capitalist countries, of course, we cannot see how far the United States and Swedish benefit levels are toward opposite ends of the range of variation. However, it seems that the United States is probably at or near the low end of the scale even with respect to retirement benefits, which can presumably be regarded as the aspect of welfare state institutions that has been more fully developed than any other in the United States.

SUMMARY

The data in terms of which the foregoing comparisons have been made are admittedly fragmentary, but they are consistent with widely held impressions concerning differences between the United States and Sweden as well as other advanced industrial countries of Western Europe. It is doubtful that the much more comprehensive comparative analysis it would certainly seem valuable to make would result in a substantially different picture. Thus, what we can probably say with reasonable confidence, however tentatively, is that the full employment-welfare state pattern of policy is approximated to a lesser degree in the United States than in any of the other countries in the group to which it belongs, at least in Western Europe, and that it is approximated to a greater degree in Sweden than in many if not most of the countries in the group, at least with respect to many of the dimensions of variation in terms of which the pattern of policy can be gauged. If it is accepted that there probably are these variations in the patterns of economic policy pursued within the plural party capitalist group, with the United States and Sweden at or near the opposite ends of the range of variation in most of the dimensions of policy in question, we can go on to explore some of the lines of inquiry through which the political factors that may help to account for these variations might be established.

III. THE POLITICAL CONTEXT OF ECONOMIC POLICY IN THE UNITED STATES

INSTITUTIONAL FRAGMENTATION

When President Kennedy was struggling to get his 1963 tax-cut proposal through Congress, he observed with envy the ease with which that instrument of demand management could be used by a government in Britain. In his words (Sundquist, 1968: 54-55), "The British prepared, proposed, passed and put into effect a proportionately larger tax cut than ours, and are getting the benefits from it, while we are still holding hearings." As James L. Sundquist points out, the President thereby "defined a fundamental problem." The problem Sundquist was referring to was the one posed by the distinctive institutional structure of government in the United States. The obstacles which that structure places in the way of using fiscal policy to maintain full employment undoubtedly have to be taken into account in any attempt to understand why unemployment levels have been higher in the United States than in Britain, Sweden, or Western Europe generally. There the structures of government generally seem to concentrate authority over the whole budgetary process in such a way as to make it much easier to use the budget to manage aggregate demand than in what Richard E. Neustadt (1960: 33) has described as our system of "separated institutions sharing powers."

The ways in which "powers" are shared among separated institutions in the United States are, of course, familiar. Authority over taxing and spending is not only shared among three separately institutionalized centers of power, the presidency, the House of Representatives, and the Senate. Authority over the two sides of the budgetary decision-making process is also split apart within each of the two legislative arenas. In addition, each side of the budgetary process is further fragmented among different sets of committees and subcommittees in the two houses of Congress.[10]

But demand management evidently cannot work by fiscal policy alone, even if it can overcome these handicaps of fragmentation. No matter what position is taken in the controversies over how much money matters, the need for coordinating monetary with fiscal policy would presumably not be denied. Yet, that coordination would also seem to be made inherently more difficult here than in Western Europe by the much greater autonomy that our central has from those politically responsible for economic policy than central banks there typically have.[11] Thus, as Sundquist (1968: 55) puts it, "Economic policy is placed in part outside the democratic process," by the Federal Reserve Board's control of monetary policy.

These are only the most obvious ways in which control over the instruments of economic policy are fragmented in the United States, but they probably establish the fundamental conditions for the fragmentation that can be traced further through the maze of executive agencies and legislative committees and the clusters of relationships formed among some of them and their particular extragovernmental constituencies.

The divisions of authority over economic policy instruments at the national level are, of course, compounded by the divisions institutionalized by federalism. This is not simply, or perhaps not even primarily, a matter of obstacles to adjusting fiscal policy to manage aggregate demand. It seems to be at least as much a matter of difficulties in the way of adjusting the flow of funds through the public sector to perform welfare state functions. The economic process has long been integrated nationally. But political authority over policies capable of modifying and offsetting the effects on individuals of participation in and dependence on that economic process remains fragmented among a multiplicity of state and local units as well as federal agencies. These units have widely varied capacities for responding to the differential regional and local impacts of decisions by firms and individuals responding largely to national and, in some degree, international markets. To be sure, the consequences of federalism vary with different types of welfare state functions, with retirement pensions in the form of Social Security nationalized to the highest degree while provision of other forms of income maintenance and particularly collective services like education is highly dispersed.[12]

All of these ways in which authority over the techniques for implementing a full employment welfare state pattern of policy is fragmented in the United States can be seen as manifestations of what Samuel P. Huntington (1968: 93-139) has referred to as the "archaic" character of American governmental institutions. As he puts it, the United States still has very much a "Tudor polity." Huntington points out that the colonists transplanted to America the institutions of English government at a time when they still retained many of the medieval characteristics that prevented the concentration of "sovereignty" in any national authority. Since that time, the structure of government in England and the rest of Europe has been "modernized." While the process has occurred in different ways, it is said to have been generally characterized by the "rationalization of authority," the "centralization of power," and the "functional differentiation" of governmental institutions. In the United States, on the other hand, this process has not gone very far. In effect, it still has a polity without sovereignty even though its economy and society have undergone rapid modernization. Thus, in Huntington's (1968: 129) estimation, "The United States ... combines the world's most modern society with one of the world's most antique polities." He explains this essentially on the grounds that "external security and internal consensus have been the principal factors militating against the modernization of American political institutions." Whatever may have been the case in the past, Huntington (1968: 133) recognizes that such factors do not seem to be operative any longer.

The political institutions suited to a society which did not have to worry about external dangers may be inappropriate for one continually involved in a balance of terror, cold war, and military interventions in distant portions of the globe. So also, the problems of race relations and poverty strengthen demands for action by the national government. The needs of national defense and social reform could undermine the traditional pluralism inherited from the past and hasten the centralization of authority and structural differentiation in American political institutions.

Perhaps, then, the generally perceived contrast between American and European governmental institutions that Huntington draws in such sweeping historical terms provides us with a sufficient explanation for the observed differences in the degree to which the full employment welfare state is approximated in America and Western Europe: the distinctive structure of governmental institutions in the United States simply makes it much harder to do so here than there.

However, this could hardly be the whole explanation, even though it is undoubtedly a part of it. As we all know, the question of how much governmental structure matters is debated among political scientists rather as the question of how much money matters is debated among economists—although it is not clear who the political scientists' Milton Friedman would be. As in the case of money, it is hard to deny that governmental structure does matter. But in both cases, other things obviously matter too, and how they interact with money and governmental structure, respectively, are essential issues for investigation.

DECENTRALIZED PARTIES

Among the other things that obviously matter a great deal are political parties. The problem defined by President Kennedy when he commented on the ease with which his British counterparts could implement an expansionary tax cut would seem to be as much a problem posed by the character of American political parties as by the institutional structure of American government. Those politically responsible for economic policy in Britain could act together with such enviable speed not simply because the "modernization" of British governmental institutions concentrates authority entirely in those who can command a majority in just one arena, a House of Commons that virtually amounts to a unicameral legislature. The operative reason why the Conservative government in office at the time could act as it did was, after all, the fact that it consisted of a group in control of an organization through which it was enabled to have the requisite majority at its disposal. In other words, as is very well known, what directly makes the structure of government in Britain function as it does is the kind of party organizations that operate in the British political arena, and the fact that one or another of them has typically been able to mobilize sufficient electoral support for candidates that can be effectively bound to vote together in the Commons to control that body, and thereby the whole policy authorizing process. With parties and political cleavages like, say, those in the French Fourth Republic, the British governmental structure would presumably function a lot more like the essentially similar structure of the French Fourth Republic.[13]

This, of course, is not simply a matter of the number of political parties. For example, both the bicameral structure of the Swedish parliament and the number of parties in it remained the same over a long period, but there was a major change in the degree of cabinet stability and the locus of power during the 1930s. During the 1920s in Sweden, there was a high degree of cabinet instability, with a succession of relatively short-lived minority and coalition governments. Under these conditions, power in the legislative arena tended to be diffused among parliamentary committees, the leading members of which evidently exercised decisive influence over policy and the fate of cabinets. At the same time, the state bureaucracy apparently enjoyed a high degree of autonomy.[14] This is admittedly an oversimplified picture, but in terms of both of its main features, it suggests that the Swedish polity at that time functioned more like the French Third and Fourth Republics than like the British polity in recent times. However, the Swedish policy-making process came to work much more like the British once the leadership of a single party proved capable of gaining parliamentary majorities or near-majorities in both chambers of parliament. As it happened, the leadership of only one party, the Social Democratic Party, has been able to do so. It has thereby succeeded in staying in office almost continuously for four decades, even though its parliamentary base has often been extremely precarious.[15] Perhaps what has happened in the French Fifth Republic is also the emergence of a single "hegemonic" party alongside a multiplicity of minority parties.[16] With De Gaulle's passing from the scene, the ability of the Gaullists to sustain such a party may well be what determines whether the Fifth Republic continues to function as it does or functions instead a good deal more like its predecessors despite the substantially different structure of its governmental institutions.

By the same token, it seems reasonable to suppose that American governmental institutions would function differently if American parties were different from what they are. Thus, if John F. Kennedy had been the head of a leadership group in a party capable of holding together a legislative majority like the British Conservative Party leadership whose power he envied, he obviously would have been spared the frustrations he experienced in getting his fiscal policy authorized. Conceivably, of course, under the conditions in which such a party could exist, the substance of the policy might have been different as well. An expansionary budget deficit might have been opened up primarily by expenditure increases rather than the tax cuts of the sort Kennedy sought and that Britain's Conservative government implemented in 1963. But this is to anticipate our later discussion.

Whatever might have been, the fact is that, "What the Constitution separates our political parties do not combine" (Neustadt, 1960: 33). It may be that the constellation of offices created by the Constitution does make it too hard for parties to achieve cohesion among their nominal adherents in those offices. The familiar implications of that constellation of offices for party organization are conveniently summarized by Neustadt (1960: 33-34):

> The parties themselves are composed of separated organizations sharing public authority. The authority consists of nominating powers. Our national parties are confederations of state and local party institutions, with a headquarters that represents the White House, more or less, if the party has a president in office. These confederacies manage presidential nominations. . . . All other nominations are controlled within the states. The President and congressmen who bear one party's label are divided by dependence upon different sets of voters. The differences are sharpest at the stage of nomination. The White House has too small a share in nominating congressmen, and Congress has too little weight in nominating Presidents for party to erase their constitutional separation. Party links are stronger than is frequently supposed, but nominating processes assure the separation.

Neither "separation of powers" nor federalism alone would seem to necessarily preclude the existence of parties centralized enough to control governments. In combination, however, they may set up obstacles to party centralization and opportunities for party decentralization that may be virtually impossible to offset under any circumstances. But it is hard to be sure. Much has happened to reinforce the evidently decentralizing impact of the constellation of offices, while some things that might have blunted that impact have not happened. What some of these things are is suggested in work that has been done by Walter Dean Burnham (1971, 1970, 1967, 1965) on what he refers to as the "decomposition" of political parties in the United States. His analysis raises questions concerning the consequences of what has happened to American political parties for the pattern of economic policy in this country that are central to our concerns, so it seems worthwhile to review that analysis in some detail.

PARTY DECOMPOSITION AND ELECTORAL DISAGGREGATION

Over seven decades, Burnham argues, there has been a decline in the extent to which American parties mobilize and structure the electorate. The trends in electoral behavior on which he bases this view are neither steady nor entirely unambiguous but they present a fairly consistent picture overall. Of these, as he says, "probably the best known," is the trend in national voter turnout. Mean turnout in presidential years dropped from 78.5% during 1876-1896 to 64.8% during 1900-1916—that is, before the adoption of the Nineteenth Amendment—and reached a low of 51.7% during 1920-1928, rising somewhat to 60.3% during 1948-1960. It has fluctuated at slightly over that level during the 1960s, thus remaining substantially below late nineteenth-century United States and current West European levels. Off-year turnout has been even lower, with trend movements parallel to presidential-year turnout (Burnham, 1965: 10-11).

As the level of participation has declined, Burnham shows, so too has the degree of partisanship among those who still participate. One measure of this is the growth of ticket-splitting that is reflected in an increasing proportion of divergent outcomes in concurrent presidential and congressional elections. As Burnham (1970: 108-109) reads the data:

> A clear pattern of electoral disaggregation emerges. At first almost nonexistent, it rises steeply during the second decade of this century and peaks temporarily in the 1920s. It then falls rapidly (but probably only to the levels of the 1910-20 period rather than to earlier ones) during the New Deal era, but once again resumes upward movement in the 1950s and reaches record highs during the 1960s.

Survey data on straight-ticket voting and party identification is only available for the most recent decades, but those that Burnham (1970: 120-121) cites are consistent with his view of electoral disaggregation.

Burnham's ultimate concern is with the significance of these trends in electoral behavior for the functions that political parties perform in the political system as a whole. As he sees it, the trends are part of a large pattern of "decomposition and contraction of those partisan structures and functions which reached their widest, most cohesive form in the decades after the Civil War" (Burnham, 1970: 131). As examples of the declining role of parties in the policy-making process, Burnham cites two indicators of the increasing importance of seniority in determining the leadership structure of the House of Representatives. One shows that the percentage of House committee chairmanships assigned on the basis of seniority grew from less than 40 prior to the turn of the century to nearly 100 since the mid-twentieth century (Burnham, 1970: 100-104). The other shows a marked increase during the twentieth century in the number of years that Speakers of the House had served in that body prior to election to that office. The mean tenure of Speakers at the time of election rose from around eight years in the decades prior to the turn of the century to well over twenty years in recent decades (Burnham, 1970: 104-106).

In general, however, Burnham's systematic analysis is confined largely to electoral behavior, and the data on trends in House leadership only illustrate the decomposition of party within the policy-making process. Thus, in the studies cited, Burnham only suggests what the broader pattern of political dynamics of which the electoral behavior is a part might be. He finds a crucial clue to the pattern in the period when the trends he discerns begin, the years just prior to the turn of the century. Burnham holds that these were years in which the business elites who were managing America's industrialization became particularly vulnerable to "an anti-industrialist assault" by those subjected to the dislocations and deprivations accompanying industrialization. In this respect, industrialization in America evoked the kind of resistance and resentment that it has everywhere, in varying degrees, "whether managed by capitalists or commissars." Accordingly, the "industrializing elites" everywhere have had to have "adequate insulation . . . from mass pressures" and the threat of "displacement by a coalition of those who are damaged" by the process of industrialization. The insulation needed to enable the process to go on has been provided in a variety of ways. These include a "totalitarian monopoly of political power in the hands of Communist industrializing elites," "less coercive . . . single-party systems of personalist dictatorship," and "the persistence of feudal patterns of deference and especially the restriction of the right to vote to the middle and upper classes" that largely served the purpose for "19th-century European elites." There were no functional equivalents in America, however, for "the institutions of mass democratic politics and universal suffrage uniquely came into being *before* the onset of full-scale industrialization." This did not pose an imminent threat during the immediate post-Civil War decades, insofar as the two major parties which succeeded in mobilizing the mass electorate to a very high degree had both come to be largely dominated by the industrializing elites themselves. But such domination as they had was insecure. There was the possibility that one of the parties could be captured by a coalition of the discontented, prefigured perhaps by the Populist movement.

> In consequence, the American industrializing elites were, and felt themselves to be, uniquely vulnerable to an anti-industrialist assault which could be carried out peacefully and in the absence of effective legal or customary sanctions by a citizenry possessing at least two generations' experience with political democracy [Burnham, 1965: 24].

This vulnerability was intensified when the depression that began in 1893 rendered chronic discontents acute, with the threat of a major political challenge becoming real when the "agrarian insurgents" took over the Democratic Party in 1896. Instead of forging a successful "coalition of the dispossessed," however, the Bryan candidacy helped to establish precisely the insulation that the industrializing elites needed but had lacked. Essential to this result was the fact that workers in the industrialized Northeast switched massively from the Democrats to the Republicans, producing a major realignment along sectional lines. The onset of the depression during a Democratic administration evidently initiated the switch; Bryan's campaign reinforced it both by its "nostalgic" agrarian appeals and the nativist overtones of its hostility to the ethnically heterogeneous Northeast; and the experience of economic recovery during the McKinley administration consolidated it. While the immediate consequence of the realignment was that it brought victory to the party that remained under the control of the industrializing elites, it had a number of consequences that reduced their political vulnerability over the longer run. Republican control of national government facilitated the transformation of the judiciary into a means of insulating business activity from legislative restraints. The very likelihood of legislative restraints was in any case diminished by the decomposition of parties that was set in motion at the same time. The realignment itself contributed to it by sharply reducing party competition. Partisan mobilization and electoral participation was further inhibited by changes in "the rules of the game," ranging from Progressive reforms like primaries and personal registration to outright disfranchisement of Blacks in the Old Confederacy (Burnham, 1965: 25-26).

To Burnham, the establishment of this "system of 1896," as E. E. Schattschneider calls it, was a fundamental turning point in American history. It enabled this country's industrializing elites to weather the 1890s "crisis of vulnerability" and provided "a way of insulating them from mass pressures without formally disrupting the pre-existing demo-cratic-pluralist political structure, without violence and without con-spiracy" (Burnham, 1965: 25; 1970: 90, 131, 183-187). But, as reflected in the course of electoral behavior, the reduction of participation and partisanship that were the central characteristics of the system of 1896 have outlived the 1896 realignment that established it. Even the New Deal realignment, Burnham argues, "did not terminate or even reverse the dispersion of the potential resources of the public sector" that those trends entailed. He recognizes (1970: 111, 131-132) that:

> The New Deal era was a time in which political power was reallocated, shifting somewhat from the hands of the business elite and its political ancillaries to a more pluralist, welfare-oriented coalition of elites and veto groups. . . . To that extent, parties resumed a good deal of their former importance as *instruments of collective social action.* This meant that not only the identity of individual office holders and the distribution of symbolic benefits but their role as a significant influence over the contours of public policy were at stake.

Nevertheless, he contends (1970: 132), "partisan organization and processes seem scarcely to have changed at all" during the New Deal era. The New Deal realignment had been unable to alter the fact that:

> The Democratic Party and electoral politics in general had become very blunt instruments for governing or generating the power links needed to coordinate the presidency and Congress as component parts of the national policy-making process [Burnham, 1970: 111].

> While . . . party as an instrument of broadly national, collective initiatives was restored during the 1932-48 period, at no time during that period did new organizational forms of party emerge. Such forms might have served as a crystallized, action-oriented definition of party as an open system of action in which the many who were individually powerless could pursue collective political objectives under elites identified with them. But they did not, and it seems very likely that under American conditions, even at the height of the Great Depression, they could not [Burnham, 1970: 132].

In short, the "process of disaggregation in policy structures inaugurated during the 1890s" continued through the New Deal virtually without interruption, while "the march toward electoral disaggregation" was resumed in the subsequent period (Burnham, 1970: 104, 132).

POLITICAL POWER IN A POLITY
WITHOUT SOVEREIGNTY

Insofar as these processes have persisted, then, they have left the United States with political parties largely incapable of serving as organizations for controlling the policy-making process—for combining "what the Constitution separates." Thus, if the American polity remains archaic, it is essentially because the kind of parties required to make the structure of governmental institutions perform modern functions have failed to develop. However, Burnham's interpretation of what has happened to American political parties suggests that the coexistence of a polity without sovereignty and a highly industrialized economy has a more specific significance. If the initial consequence of the arrested development of parties was to insulate the industrializing elites from political challenge, as he contends, it seems reasonable to suppose that the continued failure of parties to develop into "instruments of collective action" has similar consequences for the successors to the industrializing elites who now manage "mature industrialism." Although this would seem to be a conclusion to which Burnham's argument clearly points, he only suggests it in general terms. As he puts it (1970: 133; 1965: 27), the only known alternative to the "concentration of political power, locally or nationally in the hands of those who already possess concentrated economic power" is the mobilization of those without concentrated economic power within a party, or parties, that can gain control of government. If that alternative has been eliminated by the decomposition of parties, it would seem to follow that political power remains concentrated in the hands of the holders of concentrated economic power.[17]

But this may be to infer too much. It might be possible for private business elites to be dominant in a polity without sovereignty without anything like the kind of concentration of political power that would operate through a hegemonic party. In the absence of parties "in which the many who are individually powerless could pursue collective political objectives," business elites would seem to have no pressing need for a party capable of governing or even for looser forms of cohesion.[18] All that may ordinarily be needed is a kind of veto power to assure that public authority is not used in ways that are generally unacceptable to most components of the business community. That the American policy-making process is shot through with points at which such veto power can be brought to bear seems to be generally agreed—this is precisely what the Tudor character of the American polity gives rise to (Sundquist, 1968: 500-511; Huntington, 1968: 109-118; Shonfield, 1965: 323-341, 333-341; Burnham, 1970: 182-186). The kinds of access that business elites have to those veto points might well be sufficient to preserve what Burnham (1970: 186-187) refers to as "the very large private-sector role in shaping authoritative allocations of resources." Perhaps the fact that the public sector share of GNP in the United States is so low—in defiance of the clear tendency for the public sector share to rise with the productivity of the economy—is a measure of the extent to which it has been possible to preserve that private sector role. Perhaps an analysis of the composition and distributive impact of the public sector share of GNP, exceptionally low as it is, as well as the pattern of economic regulation might similarly indicate the extent to which it has been possible for business elites to assure that such encroachment of public authority on the economic process as has occurred is on terms that are acceptable to them.

Thus, when the broad features of the American political economy discussed earlier are seen in the light of Burnham's analysis of the "decay of parties," the outlines of a hypothesis concerning the political conditions that have shaped the pattern of economic policy in the United States begin to emerge. We can try to formulate that hypothesis briefly as follows. In the absence of any political party independent of business elites that can, actually or potentially, establish domestic sovereignty with respect to the economy, American business elites remain effectively insulated from political challenge through the democratic process. They are consequently able to maintain a dominant role in the political economy without having to translate their economic power into political power exercised through a party that can control the government. This dominance of the American business elites, under the particular conditions that has made it possible, is what accounts for the distinctive features of economic policy observable in the United States, especially the limited degree to which the full employment welfare state pattern of policy has been approximated in the United States as compared with other highly industrialized, plural party capitalist countries.

As formulated, the hypothesis obviously rests heavily on Burnham's interpretation of the trends that he charts. Recognizing that his interpretation may not be correct in some respects, let us nevertheless assume that it is essentially correct and consider some of the further questions that would have to be answered to test the hypothesis. Among the most central questions would seem to be those concerning the extent to which business elites remain dominant in the different plural party capitalist political economies, what accounts for such variations as there may be in the extent of business elite dominance, and the extent to which such variations account for the observable differences in patterns of economic policy. Answers to such questions would require a comprehensive comparative analysis of the politics of economic policy in the relevant group of countries. It would not be possible to even begin such an analysis within the confines of a short paper. Indeed, it might not be possible to carry it out on a much more substantial scale yet, for it is doubtful that sufficient research has been done. It may, nevertheless, be useful to explore some of the questions raised by the hypothesis and some of the lines of inquiry through which the answers might be sought. In the process, it may at least be possible to provide some firmer grounds for believing that the hypothesis is sufficiently plausible, or points to sufficiently important problems, to be worth further investigation.

IV. THE POLITICAL FUNCTIONS OF LABOR
MOVEMENT PARTIES

INDUSTRIALIZING ELITES AND POLITICAL PARTIES

A central premise underlying Burnham's interpretation, as we have seen, is that industrializing elites need insulation from the mass pressures arising in reaction to the impact of industrialization. Drawing explicitly on the general sociology of industrialization elaborated by Clark Kerr and his associates, Burnham clearly accepts such insulation as a kind of functional imperative of industrialization As the examples he cites indicate, this common imperative has been met in different ways. However, it will be recalled, he argues that the particular political mechanism through which the insulation was provided in the United States—the decay of parties—has persisted beyond the period when it was a functional imperative into mature industrialism. This, according to the hypothesis that was then advanced, is what has enabled business elites to retain a dominant position in the American political economy. If this is the case, to what extent have the political mechanisms that have performed equivalent functions for industrializing elites in other countries likewise persisted? For our purposes, the question can be confined to the other countries now in the plural party capitalist group.[19]

It seems fairly evident that the course of political development in most of those other countries has significantly affected the political mechanisms that could be said to have provided insulation for their industrializing elites, substantially modifying or even eliminating the mechanisms involved. The drastic transformations that the political system has undergone in Germany provides an extreme case in point. There, in the language of Kerr et al. (1960: 52-55), the industrializing elites included an important "dynastic" component that was completely deprived not only of insulation but of all political power by subsequent political development. But the middle-class component, which can be referred to less evasively as capitalist or at least private business, survived the drastic vicissitudes of German history. Their successors are now the managers of mature industrialism in Germany as in the other plural party capitalist countries. [20] To what extent have they and their counterparts elsewhere been able to remain dominant in the respective political economies, through the development of alternative political mechanisms to replace those which had originally insulated the industrializing elites but which have since been deprived of their efficacy? To the extent that contemporary business elites retain degrees of dominance equivalent to that exercised by their industrializing predecessors, what has made it possible? And if they have lost such degrees of dominance, on what does the extent to which they have lost it depend?

As Burnham's discussion suggests, the answers to these questions are likely to be found in large part in a comparative analysis of the development of political parties. While such an analysis cannot be undertaken here, we can perhaps suggest what it might tell us, thereby elaborating a little more specifically the hypothesis to be explored. What such an analysis would probably show is that the growth of organized labor has provided the single most important basis for the development of parties independent of business elites. For a party to be able to challenge the political power that those "who already possess concentrated economic power" can sustain, it must obviously have its own sources of the financial and organizational resources needed to mobilize electoral support. As industrialization runs its course, it would seem that the most significant sources of such resources other than the business elites themselves are the unions whose development has been the typical concomitant of industrialization.

There have unquestionably been many lines of cleavage other than class along which parties have been able to mobilize support, and various sources of personnel, funds, and organizational structures on which parties have drawn other than unions (Lipset and Rokkan, 1967: 1-64). Moreover, as Burnham points out with respect to the Southern and Western cash-crop farmers who flocked to Bryan's banner, there are various groups other than industrial workers who may be motivated to react against the process of industrialization and its various repercussions. But, as is well known, the impact of the process on groups like farmers and small proprietors in manufacturing and commerce is to reduce their proportion in the population as a whole. The proportion of industrial workers, on the other hand, rises steadily over a long period before it too starts to decline, marking the approach of what is being called postindustrial society.

The increasing unionization of the growing proportion of industrial workers in the labor force has generally tended to be related to the development of political parties that define industrial workers as their distinctive constituency, with unions providing the principal organizational channels and financial means for mobilizing that constituency (Kassalow, 1969: 5-49; Epstein, 130-166). There have, of course, been very wide variations in the development of union-party relationships, over time and within as well as among different countries. Thus, there have been differences in the order in which union and party organization has developed, the extent and forms of the links between unions and parties, the degree of cohesion or division among structures of worker mobilization, and the like. All of these variations have obviously been influenced by the distinctive configurations of factors in the particular national environments of developing labor movements. Among the most important of these have certainly been the responses of economic, governmental, and other established elites and also the presence of other popular movements organized along different occupational lines or issues. The choice of strategies adopted by party as well as union leaders in response to the opportunities and constraints created by these forces in their environments have in turn had important consequences for the extent and character of the development of union-party political formations.[21] The result, so far, has been substantial variation in the extent to which organized labor provides the basis for political parties independent of business elites and in the capacity of such labor-movement parties to influence or control governmental policy formation.

To proceed with the line of inquiry suggested by the hypothesis, it would be necessary to specify these variations as precisely as possible. First we would have to establish the variations in the different kinds of resources of power that organized labor provides in the countries with which we are concerned. Then we would have to map the variations in the extent to which these resources are translated into specifically political forms of power—that is, into resources that are brought to bear in the electoral and policy-making arenas. Ultimately, we would have to see how much difference, if any, variations in the strength of the labor movement organizations, in both the labor market and the political arenas, actually make to the patterns of economic policy that are pursued.

THE POLITICAL RESOURCES OF LABOR MOVEMENTS

How would we go about it and what could we expect to find? The first of the three steps is probably the easiest, although it is not free of difficulties. The most obvious comprehensive measure of the resources mobilized by organized labor is the proportion of total union membership in the total labor force—a measure of density of organization. For our purposes, we should have comparable series for all of the countries with which we are concerned going back over the whole period of their industrialization. Here, we can only illustrate what the comparisons would probably show by providing data for selected countries for the early 1960s, about the middle of the period to which we refer most of the data on patterns of economic policy cited earlier. Even for these relatively recent years, the data are not strictly comparable because, among other things, membership means different things in different countries. But the resulting biases run in opposite directions. In terms of solid, dues-paying membership—which obviously matters a great deal so far as the funds at the unions' disposal are concerned—the French and Italisn figures probably exaggerate. On the other hand, in terms of "psychic affiliation"—the extent to which workers identify themselves with the labor movement and will go out on strike or vote for left parties—the French and perhaps the Italian figures may well underestimate the numbers mobilizable.

Keeping these qualifications in mind, we can see what the range of variation in the density of union organization is in the seven Western countries listed in Table 4. As indicated in column 3, density is by far the highest in Sweden and lowest in France, with the United States near but not at the low end of the range of variation. Insofar as density is a measure of it, then, the electoral base that American unions can provide for a political party is among the smallest in proportion to the total electorate. Of course, there are a number of factors affecting the ability of unions to mobilize that electoral base, among which the financial resources at their disposal are naturally very important. That is consequently an important kind of data to get, but it would only be meaningful in relation to the funds available for electoral, as well as other political purposes, from other sources, particularly business elites. In the absence of a systematic comparison of all the relevant indicators, the density data provide at least a rough basis for comparing the relative electoral potential of organized labor in the different countries. On this basis, it seems reasonable to conclude that organized labor in the United States provides a smaller potential than its counterparts in most of the other countries compared.

Comparisons of the ways in which resources made available by unions

TABLE 4

ORGANIZED LABOR AND POLITICS IN THE UNITED STATES AND SIX WEST EUROPEAN COUNTRIES IN THE EARLY SIXTIES

Country and Year of Data (1)	Total Labor Force (1,000) (2)	Percentage of Total Labor Force in Unions		Largest Federation		Total Percentage of Votes for All Left/Labor Parties in Legislative Elections Nearest to Year of Other Data	
		All Unions (3)	Largest Federation (4)	Name (Initials) (5)	Party Affiliation[a] (6)	Before (7)	After (8)
Sweden, 1960	3,244	60	46	LO	Soc. Dem.	52	53
United Kingdom, 1961	24,617	40	34	TUC	Labor	44	44
West Germany, 1963	27,000[b]	29	24	DGB	Soc. Dem.	36	39
Italy, 1960	20,000	29[b]	14[b]	CGIL	Communist	41	45
Netherlands, 1963	4,400[b]	27	12	NVV	Labor	35	34
United States, 1960	72,142	25	21	AFL-CIO	?	?	?
France, 1963	20,000[b]	13[b]	8[b]	CGT	Communist	34[c]	35[c]

SOURCES: Column 1: U.S. Department of Labor (1971: 349-351). Columns 3-5: Sweden, Hadenius et al. (1969: 313); United Kingdom, Pelling (1963: 263); West Germany and Netherlands, Kassalow (1969: 88); Italy, Edelman and Fleming (1965: 11); France, Caire (1971: 334-335) and Hayward (1966: 179). Column 6: Kassalow (1969: 29-63). Columns 7 and 8: Sweden, Hadenius et al. (1969: 287); United Kingdom, Butler and King (1966: 296); West Germany and Italy, Henig and Pinder (1969: 67, 254); Netherlands, Dahl (1966: 423); France, Ehrmann (1968: 211).

a. Includes informal affiliations.
b. Estimated.
c. First ballot.

are translated into resources for political actors in the process that determines how public authority is used are considerably more problematical. The obvious difference between the United States and all the other countries is that there is no party based financially, organizationally, and electorally primarily on unions and the working class generally. Looking just at the European cases, there are large variations in the extent to which even Left parties can actually be said to be labor movement parties in that sense, and in the degree of political power that more or less genuinely labor movement parties have attained. The percentage of votes cast for the European Left or labor movement parties provides a first approximation of their political power. Such data for elections to national legislatures in the nearest years before and after the years for which union density are provided are presented in columns 7 and 8 of Table 4. The percentages are for the combined votes of parties variously designated as labor, social democratic, socialist, and communist. The differences in electoral support for the parties correspond roughly with the differences in the density of union membership except that the range of variation in electoral support is narrower. Without going into the reasons for this, one thing that should be pointed out is that unions in several of the countries belong to central federations with specific religious identities and which serve to some extent to mobilize support for similarly identified parties as opposed to the Left parties. In the major cases of Christian Democratic parties in Germany and Italy, of course, the parties are broad, cross-class parties with support from business elites.[22]

The religious, ideological, and occupational cleavages among the parties that more or less parallel such divisions in organized labor naturally have important consequences for the ways in which the parties' electoral support can be converted into bargaining power in or control of the policy-making process. The relative weakness of the French and Italian left has evidently been a function of the fundamental and persistent division between strong communist and somewhat weaker non-communist formations which is not present elsewhere. Other divisions do occur elsewhere, however. An indication of the degree of division at the central union federation level is provided by column 4 of Table 4 which shows the proportion of the labor force in unions affiliated to the largest central federations, which are communist led in the French and Italian cases.

The variations in the political power attained by labor movement or left parties in terms of influence on policy are presumably more adequately reflected by variations in their participation in governments than by voting statistics. In these terms, the Swedish Social Democratic Party has obviously attained the most power, having governed alone or in coalition for four decades, with an interruption of only a few months in 1936. In addition, it formed minority governments or participated in coalitions for a total of six years prior to the beginning of its long reign in 1932. The other Scandinavian labor movement parties have also experienced long periods in office, alone or in coalition, although not for as many years as the Swedish Social Democrats. Outside of Scandinavia, only the British Labor Party has had sufficient strength to form a government by itself for any length of time. Most of the other parties of the same type in Western Europe have participated in coalition governments at some time or another, with the German Social Democratic Party having the most experience as senior partner in coalitions, including the Weimar period. The Left parties in France and Italy have been weakest in terms of participation in government.

When we try to extend this comparison to the United States we run into difficulties. What do we say in view of the fact there is no equivalent in the United States to the separate Left or labor parties whose political power in Europe we have been comparing? The zeros in column 7 and 8 might simply be taken to indicate that in the absence of such a party, the resources that organized labor makes available perform no function in American politics equivalent to that which such resources perform in Europe. But this would be patently absurd in view of the increasing importance of unions within the Democratic Party. A number of observers have noted this development and J. David Greenstone has recently analyzed it in great detail. In his view, there has been a considerable degree of convergence between the union-Democratic Party relationship in the U.S. and union-party relationships in Western Europe. With respect to the American case, he summarizes this tendency as follows (Greenstone, 1969: 361-361):

> In the early and mid-1960s, the American labor movement's role in the national Democratic Party represented a partial equivalence to the Social Democratic (formerly socialist) party-trade union alliances in much of Western Europe. This equivalence obtained with respect to its activities as a party campaign (and lobbying) organization, its influence as a party faction, and its welfare-state objectives.

Greenstone is careful to stress the limitations of this development. If "union financial contributions accounted for a sizable fraction—about one-fourth—of all Democratic campaign funds in national elections," that left three-fourths to be financed elsewhere. While "the national labor movement became one of several important, largely autonomous party factions that influenced party decisions and most party leaders" the other factions remained important. Furthermore, "By comparison with European socialist branch organizations, the congressional district COPE structure had fewer strongly motivated members, was less able to sustain continuous activity, and was less successful in covering all working-class districts." Although American labor's political goals have expanded from narrow pressure group protection to broad "welfare-state programs that sought to benefit lower-class citizens, many of whom were not affiliated with the labor movement," these goals have been "less extensive than the welfare program actually enacted in many European countries" (Greenstone, 1969: 362-363). Finally, after explaining why American labor's partisan role has grown, Greenstone (1969: 365) sums up the reasons for the limitations on that growth:

> Organized labor's partisan role—as a channel for collectivist working class demands with a lower capacity to convert such demands into issues than comparable European union-party formations—was thus a function of the superimposition of an industrial economic order on a deeply entrenched democratic, pro-capitalist, federal political regime.

Thus, Greenstone's judicious discussion suggests that organized labor in the United States does in fact perform functions in American politics that are in significant respects equivalent to the functions performed by its West European counterparts. Indeed, it may be noted, the growth in labor's partisan role that he stresses suggests the possibility of a reversal of the decomposition of parties that Burnham describes, although the present flux in Democratic Party politics would seem to make any predictions hazardous. In any case, Greenstone's analysis suggests at the same time that American labor's capacity to perform such functions, and the impact it accordingly has in the electoral and policy-making arenas, are significantly less than those of organized labor in much of Western Europe. This, of course, is consistent with the impression given by such indicators as we have referred to earlier.

Admittedly, it remains difficult and even perhaps misleading to try to say just where American unions are on the different dimensions of variation in terms of which we suggested it was possible to compare the political power that organized labor can sustain. Nevertheless, if we could conceive of a scale on which the labor movements in our group of countries could be arranged in order of the political power they can sustain, it seems clear that the Swedish labor movement would provide the limiting case toward the end of the scale at which that political power is greatest, while the American labor movement would lie fairly far toward the other end of the scale, without necessarily providing the limiting case toward that end. The main reason for thinking so is that American labor's partisan role is that of a component in a cross-class party in which business elites in particular also have significant roles, perhaps not unlike the Christian Democratic Party of Germany. The parallel may not be an appropriate one, but the point is that American labor is still not part of a party independent of business elites. Instead, it is part of a coalition in which it has to bargain no less than those European labor movement parties that have to bargain within coalitions when the limits on their electoral strength leave them no alternative. However, the evaluation of the bargaining power of various partners in complex and shifting coalitions is one of the most difficult things for social scientists to do, especially when the whole game is played in several arenas in which the distribution of relevant resources among the partners is different. To go beyond what can be said on the basis of the distribution of political resources, it is necessary to proceed to the third step and see what we are likely to find if we try to see what relationships there may be between the apparent differences in labor movement functions in the various party systems and the observable variations in patterns of policy.

POLITICAL STRATEGY AND THE WELFARE STATE

We certainly could not expect to find any simple, straightforward relationship between the kinds of resources in terms of which we have compared labor movement political formations and variations in the patterns of economic policy that may be observed. The development of welfare state institutions may nevertheless have been some kind of function of the growth of labor movement or Left parties. In the comparative analysis of Social Security programs cited earlier, Aaron (1967: 17) finds a strong positive correlation between the age of such programs and their size relative to national income. He then observes:

> The political complexion of the governments in power when social security programs are first introduced is usually rather similar. Moderately leftist governments, which come to power on promises of social reform, take the first steps.

This would lead us to expect that the countries with the oldest (and consequently largest) programs are those in which "moderately leftist" governments came to power earliest. However, this is not the case.

Aaron identifies the programs enacted in "Germany and Austria in the 1880's" as the earliest ones. This undoubtedly helps to account for the fact that the present programs in those countries are among the largest, but the Hohenzollern and Hapsburg regimes under which the programs were inaugurated were hardly moderately leftist. Whatever may have been the case as far as Austria was concerned, Germany's priority in the history of welfare state institutions had its source in an effort to reinforce precisely that political mechanism for insulating its combination of dynastic and middle-class industrializing elites against mass pressures referred to earlier. In its German version, that mechanism depended on Bismarck's ability to carry out his audacious grand strategy for combining the forms of mass political participation—through universal male suffrage—and the substance of an authoritarian political system in which the power to govern remained independent of the outcome of elections (Holborn, 1969: 194-297). Bismarck saw the small but rapidly growing Social Democratic Party as a threat to that strategy. It seems agreed that the social insurance legislation enacted at Bismarck's initiative constituted one of two elements in his effort to meet that threat. The other element, of course, was repression; although, as Hajo Holborn (1969: 287) points out, it definitely involved "a milder form of suppression than that adopted by the French government after the Paris Commune of 1871."

Whether it was because neither social policy nor repression were carried far enough or not, they failed to produce their intended result. This evidently contributed to Bismarck's conclusion that his grand strategy was unworkable and that it was therefore necessary to engineer a coup d'etat against his own constitution. Although he was removed from the scene before he could resort to such a remedy, conservative elites entertained the possibility of resorting to it on subsequent conditions (Holborn, 1969: 300-301, 323; Röhl, 1967: 50-55, 110-117, 200-222). A variant of it was finally employed by a coalition of traditional conservatives, business elites, and Hitler in 1933, when the latter's ability to mobilize more mass support than the former could made the project seem feasible (Bullock, 1964: 187-250). What followed, as we know, was not only the complete suppression of the union-party formation that had by then grown large, but something far different from a restoration of Bismarck's pseudo-constitutionalism or any more authoritarian version of it he might have had in mind. Nevertheless, it is important to note in the context of our discussion that the Nazi regime was very much concerned with the mobilization function that social policy could serve, relying heavily on its Labor Front to perform that function (Schoenbaum, 1967: 73-112).

This cursory review of the German experience is pertinent because it points to some of the ambiguity in the relationships between the power of the labor movement political formations and the extent to which welfare state institutions have developed. They clearly did not originate in Germany because such a political formation achieved the power needed to control public authority and use it to establish social insurance and the like. On the other hand, the emergence of such a formation was perceived as a potential threat to the political elites who were in control of public authority, and the establishment of welfare state institutions was seen by the latter as a way of coping with that threat. This was by no means unique to Germany in Bismarck's day and later. For example, it seemed like an excellent idea to Joseph Chamberlain, the British Liberal who led the migration of Britain's industrializing elites into the Conservative Party in the 1880s (Beer, 1969: 251-254, 272, 282-284). In a famous speech in 1885, it may be recalled, Chamberlain urged his listeners to recognize the need for social insurance programs by asking, "what ransom will property pay for the security it enjoys?" While he subsequently regarded his translation of the idea into English as too blunt and substituted the word "insurance" for "ransom," the reasoning remained the same (Garvin, 1932-1969: I, 549, 551).

On the other hand, the Conservative Party did not accept the logic of Chamberlain's position at the time—"social reform was not on the whole a profitable line to pursue," as the first leader of the Party to rise from the ranks of the industrializing elites is said to have seen it (Beer, 1969: 272-274). Instead, the foundations of the British welfare state were laid by the Liberal Party. This was done especially by Lloyd George's National Insurance Act of 1911, which was vigorously opposed by the Conservatives. It was precisely in this era that British labor was in the process of transition from a pressure group within the Liberal Party into a separate union-based party (Beer, 1969: 105-152). It does not seem like stretching matters too much to say that significant welfare state institutions were first established in Britain because of the political power of a coalition in which organized labor played a major role, functionally equivalent to the role American labor now plays in the Democratic Party. From Lloyd George's point of view, the enactment of social insurance legislation may well have been expected to prevent the mobilization of the working-class electorate by a separate labor movement party, much as Bismarck had hoped, and with as little success. If that was Lloyd George's expectation, it was obviously cast within the framework of a fundamentally different political strategy from that of Bismarck. Even so, both could be said to be responding, however differently, to the perceived power, actual or potential, of political elites whose principle resources of power were provided by the growth of organized labor.

Were welfare state institutions established so much later in the United States because the political resources provided by organized labor were so meager for so long? While the New Deal certainly can be said to have been a moderately leftist government, it probably conferred more strength on organized labor than organized labor provided for it. If the New Deal's social security legislation was a response to any political power that may have been perceived as a threat or opportunity, it was probably that built up by the Townsend Movement and Huey Long rather than by any labor leaders. Nevertheless, while that may have created the immediate political imperative behind the legislation, its substance had its sources in the development of social policy in states like Wisconsin in which farmer-labor politics were crucial (Leuchtenberg, 1963: 96-99, 103-114, 130-137, 150-152). Without attempting to review the American case in any detail, it does seem to suggest, as the German and British cases do, that there is a relationship between the development of welfare state institutions and the growth of labor movement political formations. At the same time, it suggests as do the other cases, that the relationship is a complex one, in which the resources that organized labor makes available for some political elites necessarily enters into the strategies adopted by others, but in a variety of different ways, contingent on very many other variables.

THE POLITICS OF EMPLOYMENT POLICY

More light may be shed on the relationship by a brief glance at some of the political conditions under which governmental responses to unemployment have varied. As we can see from Samuel H. Beer's (1969: 208-216, 302-317) illuminating analysis of the politics of British economic policy during the second world war and the early postwar years, the wartime experience of full employment was converted into a demand for full employment after the war. The Conservative leadership of the wartime coalition was reluctant to commit itself to fulfilling that demand, refusing to make William Beveridge's proposals for full employment policy an official document as it had felt compelled to do in the case of his recommendations concerning social insurance and social services, even though Beveridge himself held that the success of the latter were contingent on full employment (Beer, 1969: 212, note 3). The Labor Party, however, articulated the demand and promised to fulfill it, which undoubtedly contributed to its 1945 victory. Although it was probably more the unanticipated course of events in the international economy than the Labor government's policy that caused it, the continuation of full employment while the Labor Party was in power apparently reinforced the belief that the demand could be fulfilled and thereby established the maintenance of full employment as a political imperative.

Having won the 1951 election after a campaign in which the Labor Party warned that the Conservatives would not maintain full employment and in which the Conservatives claimed that they would, the new Conservative Government had to make good on their claim. It proved able to do so without much difficulty and the Conservatives were rewarded with a larger victory in 1955. Soon afterward, however, the second postwar Conservative government came face to face with the unemployment-inflation dilemma from which its predecessor had been largely spared. Initially, the Conservatives decided that demand could not be restricted sufficiently to curb inflationary pressures without increasing unemployment to levels that would entail too great a risk of electoral defeat to be acceptable. Thus, the Conservative Prime Minister's view in 1956 was that any significant departure from the very low levels of unemployment that had come to be defined as full employment was "politically not tolerable" (Beer, 1969: 360). However, the Conservatives proved unable to repress inflationary pressures by either a voluntary or imposed "incomes policy," nor did they seek any alternative policy aimed at the structural sources of inflationary tendencies (Beer, 1969: 362-369; Clegg and Adams, 1957: 27-34, 48-90, 142-151). Consequently, in 1957 they felt compelled to restrict demand somewhat even if it meant an increase in unemployment. Yet, as the 1959 election approached, the government reversed itself, entering the next phase of what has become the familiar "stop-go" policy cycle. In phase with the timing of elections, the cycle was continued during the third postwar Conservative government of 1959-1964 (Brittan, 1970: 207-290).

The point is that as long as the Labor Party continued to provide a credible alternative to any Conservative government that failed to maintain full employment at levels maintained during the postwar Labor government, Conservative governments had to approximately match those levels. Indeed, the more they did so, the more they reinforced those levels as a standard of performance. Conservative policy was accordingly constrained by a very strong full employment imperative at the same time that it was subjected to a recurrent and increasingly strong balance of payments imperative, as it was defined in terms of the prevailing payments system. Conservative economic policy bounced back and forth between them in the stop-go pattern that made it progressively more difficult to cope with the unemployment-inflation dilemma (Caves et al., 1968: 4-11, 34-45, 488). However, the Labor Party badly undermined its credibility as a full employment alternative by its performance when it was back in office between 1964 and 1970. By the time it was voted out in 1970, the Wilson government had allowed unemployment to reach levels higher than any since the great Depression, having sacrificed full employment to a futile three-year effort to avoid devaluation which called up bitter memories of the MacDonald Labor government of 1929-1931.[23]

The result was to significantly relax the strength of the full employment imperative as a constraint on Conservative economic policy. The Conservative government that came into office after the 1970 election had much more room for maneuver, to which the preceding Labor government's belated devaluation and abortive initiatives in the field of industrial relations regulation also contributed. With its calculus of risks substantially altered, the Conservative government has evidently felt free to let unemployment rise even higher, although its most recent budget was designed to reduce it somewhat.[24] Meanwhile, a group of Conservative MPs, including some who have since become Ministers, have explicitly articulated a lower level of aspirations with respect to full employment as an appropriate one for policy to meet.[25]

Failure on the part of party leaders to recognize what can be done to cope with substantive policy problems consistently with their own stakes and those of their supporters can have major consequences. The responses of labor movement party elites in Germany, Britain and Sweden to the great Depression provide striking examples that are especially pertinent. In both Germany and Britain, important leaders of organized labor became convinced that it was necessary to break with balanced budget orthodoxy and mount a program of deficit financed government expenditures to cope with mass unemployment. But the leadership of both the German Social Democratic Party and the British Labor Party refused to go along.[26] In both cases, the party leaders seemed incapable of breaking out of a conceptual trap defined by their rhetorical commitment to the view that nothing but the establishment of socialism—in some remote future—could cure the ills of capitalism, and a practical commitment to the financial orthodoxy of the pre-Keynesian era.

As is well known, the consequences in the two cases were fatefully different. We cannot say that the world would have been spared the tragedy inflicted by Hitler if the German Social Democratic leaders—as well as others, of course—had abandoned their belief that budgets had to be balanced.[27] But it is obvious that a policy of deficit financed expenditures opens up possibilities for coalitions that remain closed on the balanced budget assumption. The quest for balanced budgets in a depression turns the politics of economic policy into a futile zero-sum game in which any group's benefits from government expenditures means another group's tax increases. If the Social Democratic leaders had understood the alternative that its affiliated union bureaucracy proposed, it might just have been sufficient to bring success to the last minute effort by General von Schleicher to forge a broad coalition around just such an alternative. A restoration of the working alliance between labor and the army that had operated during World War I in the winter of 1932-1933 might well have thwarted Hitler's bid for power.[28] . As it turned out, the failure of Schleicher's coalition strategy opened the way for the coalition of traditional Conservatives, business elites and the Nazis through which Hitler's dictatorship was established.

The similar failure of MacDonald's minority Labor government to break from financial orthodoxy had trivial consequences by comparison with those that ensued in Germany. However, it may have meant the loss of an opportunity for extended control of government by a left majority coalition consisting of the Labor Party and a substantial fraction of the Liberal Party (Skidelsky, 1967: 387-395). This is what seems to be suggested by what happened in Sweden. In a situation that was fundamentally similar in both economic and political respects, the Swedish Social Democrats pursued a different strategy. They gained enough parliamentary support from Agrarian Party dissidents to control the government after the 1932 election and to enact a deficit financed public works program which the Social Democrats had adopted in 1930. The initiative for breaking out of the conceptual trap in which its German and British counterparts were locked came from within the Swedish Social Democratic leadership itself rather than from the unions.[29] Perhaps this is why the leadership had the confidence to make the innovation in economic policy that the German and British labor movement party elites did not have. In any case, the Swedish Social Democrats had a program to which they could rally the necessary margin of additional support. Moreover, the program appeared to work as they insisted it would, over all the objections based on established business and academic wisdom. Actually, it was the recovery of exports rather than their economic policy that probably accounted for most of the recovery in the Swedish economy (Arndt, 1944: 212-220; Lundberg, 1957: 22-45, 54-55. However, the Social Democrats could and did claim that they had been proved right. The result was that they made substantial gains in the 1936 election and were returned to office, as they have ever since. Thus, the Swedish Social Democrats were able to enlarge the scope of their support in the later 1930s on the basis of policy and power strategies that enabled them to make the most of the support available to them in the early 1930s.

If the British Labor Party had adopted analogous strategies, they would not necessarily have achieved the same result. The difference between the opposition of a single, cohesive Conservative Party in Britain and an opposition divided within as well as among three "bourgeois" parties in Sweden, differences in timing, and any number of other differences might have precluded it. But it is hard to avoid the impression that the Swedish Social Democratic leaders have tended to make the most of the resources made available to them by the development of organized labor while the British Labor Party leaders have repeatedly squandered them.[30]

The preceding discussion only points toward some of the variables that intervene between the size and structure characteristics of organized labor and the patterns of economic policy that governments pursue. As we try to take more and more of these intervening variables into account, it becomes increasingly doubtful that any generalizations concerning the relationships between such labor movement characteristics and patterns of economic policy can be formulated. Yet, it seems impossible to dismiss the impression that differences in the political power that organized labor has been able to sustain have made an important difference in the politics of economic policy in the countries with which we are concerned, even if the difference has not been very consistent.

With respect to the United States in particular, it is hard to avoid the impression that the failure of organized labor to develop sufficiently to provide the basis for a union-party formation, at least until now, has been a decisive factor in the failure of cohesive parties to develop. In the absence of such parties, it is difficult to see what can substantially overcome the fragmented, or archaic, character of public authority in the United States. Under the circumstances, it can hardly be surprising that the role of the public sector in the American economy has lagged behind that in the industrially advanced West European countries. Moreover, under these circumstances, there seems to be little reason why the character as well as the extent of the American public sector role should not be confined largely to what has been acceptable to American business elites. Whether this has in fact been the case could only be established by a systematic analysis of the politics of economic policy in the United States over an extended period that cannot be attempted here. However, the sense in which it might be possible to say that American economic policy has been constrained by what has been acceptable to American business elites can perhaps be illustrated by turning again to President Kennedy's fiscal policy initiative.

V. FISCAL POLICY ON THE NEW FRONTIER

THE KEYNESIAN REVOLUTION: AMERICAN STYLE

The enactment of the tax cut Kennedy proposed was undoubtedly one of the most important economic policy decisions made in the postwar period—and also one of the most illuminating for our purposes. As has been abundantly observed, it marked the first time that an American government deliberately and openly implemented the Keynesian technique of expanding economic activity and reducing unemployment by actions designed to increase the government's budget deficit. In the words of Walter Heller (1967: 1-2), who was presumably most responsible for the Kennedy administration's innovation in economic policy,

> We at last accept in fact what was accepted in law twenty years ago (in the Employment Act of 1946), namely, that the Federal government has an overarching responsibility for the nation's economic stability and growth. And we have at last unleashed fiscal and monetary policy for the aggressive pursuit of those objectives.

Perhaps Heller's enthusiasm drove him to exaggerate the extent to which the innovation was a break with the past rather than a fairly short incremental step, as Herbert Stein (1969: 3-5, 454-468) seems to suggest. However, most commentators seem to agree with Heller (1967: 2) that "profound changes" were involved, recognizing that "what they have wrought is not the creation of a 'new economics,' but the completion of the Keynesian Revolution—thirty years after John Maynard Keynes fired the opening salvo."

But why did the innovation in policy come as late as it did, later than in any of the other countries in the relevant group with the possible but doubtful exception of West Germany (Shonfield, 1965: 284-289, 332-333)? And when it finally came, why did it come in the particular form that it did? Was it because Kennedy was the first president capable of being educated (in office) by Keynesian economists? If so, why were his predecessors so immune to the ideas that lay behind the Employment Act of 1946? In any case, while penetration of the presidency by those ideas was undoubtedly a necessary condition for their embodiment in practice, that was clearly not a sufficient condition. Everybody pushing for the policy innovation from Kennedy on down evidently chafed at the resistance encountered in Congress. What overcame that resistance? What changed to make possible what had previously been impossible?

BUSINESS PRIORITIES AND PRESIDENTIAL OPTIONS

The impact of Kennedy's assassination obviously made a difference, but as Sundquist and others have argued quite convincingly, the tax cut and much of Kennedy's program was already beginning to move toward enactment before the tragedy at Dallas (Sundquist, 1968: 46-52, 481-484). Furthermore, most accounts seem to agree that the decisive factor in moving the tax cut through Congress was business support for it. But business support for the tax cut reflected a basic change in the prevailing attitude among business elites toward budget deficits as an instrument of economic policy. This is evidently what changed and what made the difference. As long as business elites generally remained opposed to the use of that instrument, it could not be used. Once they turned in favor of it, it could be used.

This is not to imply unanimity in the business community, before or after the change. As Jim Heath (1969: 10) points out, "It is more accurate to speak of business *communities.*" The fact that the Committee for Economic Development has been way ahead of the National Association of Manufacturers in the economic sophistication of its positions is well known. But there can hardly be any doubt that the weight of business opinion was hostile to any version of Keynesian policy long after the widespread business opposition to it during the fight over the 1946 Employment Act that Sidney S. Alexander (1948: 177-198) documented and analyzed.[31] The shift in the center of gravity of business opinion seems to have been signaled above all by the United States Chamber of Commerce. According to Sundquist (1968: 47-48), this

> most important single business organization . . . . had in the early 1960's deserted the view that tax reductions should be made only out of surplus, and its 1962-1962 president, Ladd Plumley, was an all-out supporter of tax reduction. By the time of the Ways and Means Committee hearings, in 1963, it was joined by the National Association of Manufacturers, the American Bankers Association, the New York Stock Exchange, and an array of trade associations in testifying in favor of the measure.

The marshaling of business support was not confined to these established organizations. Apparently at the administration's initiative, the leaders of major corporations, headed by Henry Ford, II, Roger Blough, and Stuart Saunders, were mobilized on behalf of the measure in the Business Committee for Tax Reduction in 1963. In such massive business support, Sundquist (1968: 47) says, "is found the key to passage of the tax reduction measure."

Why did the weight of business opinion swing behind the Keynesian technique of expansionary budget deficits to which it had for so long been apparently opposed? A large part of the answer would seem to lie in the fact that Kennedy proposed a version of the technique that could be recognized as acceptable, or consistent with long-standing business attitudes to economic policy. If we may reduce it to its bare essentials, the basic Keynesian prescription for using fiscal policy to reduce unemployment is an increase in aggregate demand produced by an excess of government expenditures over revenues—hence a budget deficit. Whatever deficit may be regarded as necessary, it can be brought about by a wide variety of tax or expenditure changes or combinations of both. At one extreme, reliance may be placed entirely on increasing expenditures more rapidly than revenues will increase if tax rates are left unchanged. At the other extreme, reliance may be placed entirely on tax cuts to open up a gap between revenues and expenditures which may be left constant or even reduced. In between, there are any number of combinations of tax cuts and expenditure increases that can be relied on to achieve the necessary deficit. There is evidently room for quite a lot of debate over the relative expansionary efficiency of tax cuts and expenditure increases, involving their multiplier effects, incentive effects, rapidity of impact, and so on. Fundamentally, however, it would seem that the basic choice between an expenditure increase or tax cut approach is a choice for or against enlarging the public sector share of GNP.

Defined in these terms, the choice made by the Kennedy administration was essentially against enlarging the public sector share. The compelling reason for that choice seems plain: only a deficit achieved primarily through the tax cut approach could elicit the support of business elites without which no expansionary deficit at all could be enacted. That was the version of the technique that was acceptable to business. If Stein's (1969: 458) estimation of business opinion is correct—and he has presumably been in a fairly good position to gauge that opinion—businessmen have not been as opposed to budget deficits as their rhetoric would make it seem.

> The business leadership thought, as the politicians did, that there was a strong budget-balancing sentiment in the country, and they wanted to use that for beating an administration whose other policies, including both high spending and high taxes, they disliked more than deficit finance but found less easy to attack publicly.

At another point, Stein (1968: 442) reports among business leaders a "deeply felt and widely shared desire to restrain the expansion of federal activity."

Thus the issue was only partly about budget-balancing—about the relationship between revenues and expenditures. The issue was also, and mainly, about the level of both. The intention was to slow down the growth of both expenditures and revenues, as compared with their past rate and with what was believed to be the intention of the administration [Stein, 1969: 443].

Kennedy (1962) appealed to this concern of the business community in his speech to the Economic Club in New York:

The final and best means of strengthening demand among consumers and business is to reduce the burden on private income and the deterrents to private initiative which are imposed by our present tax system.

The present tax system . . . siphons out of the private economy too large a share of personal and business purchasing power. . . . [Sundquist, 1968: 43-44].

In other words, the remedy for a restrictive fiscal policy is tax cuts. The alternative of expenditure increases is ruled out. The problem is diagnosed as taxes that are too high; the possibility that it is expenditures that are too low is not entertained. In calling this speech "the most Republican speech since McKinley," John Kenneth Galbraith "may have gone too far," says Stein, suggesting that "Mellon might have been a better reference than McKinley." As Stein (1969: 421, 285) points out, Andrew Mellon had long ago argued that "tax reduction would stimulate the economy, raise the revenues, and help the budget." Whatever Kennedy had said earlier in the year about dispelling economic "myths," he was invoking a venerable ideology in his appeal to the conservative businessmen assembled before him in New York. For this writer, Kennedy's language is strikingly reminiscent of the arguments advanced by the spokesmen of Swedish business during the 1920s and deployed against the Social Democrats' expansionary budget of 1933 (Lewin, 1967: 11-22).

Wilbur Mills' speech to the House of Representatives in support of the tax cut spelled out the choice embodied in it very explicitly. He spoke of two roads to prosperity.

One is the tax reduction road. The other is the road of Government expenditure increases.

There is a big difference—a vital difference—between them. The route of Government expenditure increase . . . leads to big Government, especially big Central Government. . . . The route I prefer is the tax reduction road which gives us a higher level of economic activity and a bigger and more prosperous and more efficient economy with a larger and larger share of the enlarged activity initiating in the private sector of the economy [Stein, 1969: 449-450].

Whatever Kennedy, or for that matter Mills, may really have believed about the relative merits of the expenditure or tax-cut approaches, they were evidently in no doubt about the approach that could win enough support to be implemented. In fact, according to Stein (1969: 411), increased federal expenditures had been Kennedy's "preferred route to economic expansion" in 1961. "In the summer of 1962 he still believed that there were unmet social needs much more important than the private needs that would be satisfied by tax reduction." Within the administration, Galbraith was apparently the strongest advocate of this position. But the political basis for implementing the expenditure approach was simply not there. This was the fundamental fact of political life that evidently removed the expenditure approach from serious consideration. The AFL-CIO stressed in 1964 that it "has long urged increased government spending as the best way to create new jobs and continues to do so" (Biemiller, 1964: 14). But organized labor could not provide the political resources to sustain that approach over the objections of business elites then or at any other time. Years of lobbying by organized labor, from its efforts on behalf of much stronger language than was ultimately included in the Employment Act of 1946 down through the Kennedy years, were never enough to translate even the Act's moderate commitment in principle into policy practice. It was possible for it to happen at last only when American business elites accepted the principle and only when the principle was put into practice in a form that was acceptable to them. The AFL-CIO, like the President, bowed before the fundamental realities of power in the American political economy and settled for the tax-cut approach that put the principle in the form acceptable to business.

Nothing has happened to change the situation. As the *New York Times* (1972) account of the Brookings 1973 budget study says, "The four major tax bills of 1964, 1965, 1969 and 1971 have reduced individual, corporate and excise taxes, at 1972 levels of income, by $45 billion, only partly offset by $28 billion of increases in Social Security taxes." The fiscal dividends that Heller (1967: 34) confidently anticipated in dismissing the allocative issues raised by "our Ambassador to India" have evaporated. Shaped by the priorities of American business elites, which do leave room for military expenditures, the public sector share of GNP proves to be inadequate to any alternative set of priorities which would require a lot more room for nonmilitary expenditures. In terms of the latter, taxes are not too high, after all, but too low.

VI. CONCLUSION

The American policy-making process proved capable of delivering the kind of fiscal policy that Kennedy sought, even though it did not do so as rapidly as the British policy-making process that he admired so much. But what the American process delivered under two Democratic presidents was the same kind of fiscal policy that the British process delivered under a government controlled by the Conservative Party, the party sustained primarily by Britain's business elites. Since the two Democratic presidents were similarly dependent on the support of American business elites —certainly by necessity in Kennedy's case and possibly by design in Johnson's case—it is hardly surprising that the pattern of fiscal policy should have been similar in the British and American cases.[32] But in the American political arena, there is evidently no political formation that can make the policy-making process deliver an alternative kind of fiscal policy. In Britain, organized labor provides the basis for such a political formation. Ineffective as its leadership may frequently have been, its presence in the political arena was able to enforce a higher standard of full employment, and its maintenance by a version of fiscal policy that resulted in a higher public sector share of GNP, than in the United States throughout most of the postwar period.

The presence of labor movement political formations of varying degrees of effectiveness in Western Europe generally seems to have contributed to correspondingly similar results. Insofar as we can compare the political power that can be sustained by organized labor in all of the plural party capitalist countries, variations in that power do seem to have a relationship, however complex and uneven, to the extent to which the full employment welfare state pattern of economic policy is approximated in those countries. The relationship seems to be particularly clear in the cases that lie at or near the opposite ends of the range of variation in both power and policy, the United States, and Sweden. Perhaps the relationship is clear enough to be summed in the following tentative conclusion. Business elites seem to have been dominant in the American economic policy-making arena for a long time to something like the same degree that labor elites have been dominant in the Swedish economic policy-making arena in recent decades. Neither have consistently been in a sufficiently strong position to get the policies they wanted, but both have generally been able to determine the terms on which economic policy issues are defined and settled, and to veto terms that are unacceptable to them. If this is so, it is probably a large part of the explanation of why the patterns of economic policy in the United States and Sweden are at or near the opposite ends of the range of variation in the extent to which the full employment welfare state pattern of policy is approximated in the comparable group of countries.

NOTES

1. There are difficulties in the choice of terminology. "Western" cannot be used without excluding Japan or doing violence to both its cultural and geographic senses. Neither "capitalist" nor "advanced industrial" can be used without qualification since both are applicable to political economies in which governmental authority is not contingent on free elections. Moreover, much of the available terminology bristles with ideological connotations. While "plural party capitalist" is by no means free of difficulties, it at least leaves room for the existence or possibility of other party-economy relationships, such as single-party capitalist or plural-party socialist.

2. The expression is used by C.A.R. Crosland (1956: 61) to describe the economic and social policies pursued by both Labor and Conservative governments in Britain over the decade after World War II. He was a major "revisionist" spokesman in the Labor Party's ideological controversies during the 1950s. As such, he seems to have exaggerated the extent and invulnerability of full employment and welfare state institutions in Britain. The work of Richard M. Titmuss (1958) has been the source and stimulus for a more modest and critical assessment of the achievements of postwar British policy.

3. Sweden provides the earliest and clearest prewar case in which budgetary policy was explicitly aimed at reducing unemployment through deficit financed expenditures as well as for welfare state functions. See Arndt (1944: 207-220) and Rustow (1955: 103-109). A general discussion of policy ideas in Sweden at the time is provided in Lewin (1967: 45-175).

4. On the reduction of full employment aspirations, see discussion below, p. 45. On diverse tendencies affecting welfare state institutions, see Titmuss (1960, 1958); also Abel-Smith and Townsend (1965: 57-67). A comparative analysis is provided by Sellier (1970). Schorr (1972) raises some of the issues with respect to the American context.

5. Most of the well-known contributions to the debate over the decline or end of ideology are collected in Waxman (1968).

6. Percentages for 1950 and 1960 from Westerlind and Beckman (1965: 95); 1970 interpolated from fiscal year figures in the Swedish Budget 1969/1970 and 1970/1971 (1970: 56; 1969: 50).

7. The results of the low-income study are being reported in a number of publications, the first of which is Svenska folkets inkomster (1970).

8. The supplementary pension scheme is financed entirely by "contributions" paid by employers, or self-employed persons, on all earnings between the base amount and the maximum, at rates that have gradually been increased over the 1960s (see Uhr, 1966: 63-66).

9. The establishment of the Swedish supplementary pension scheme, enacted by one vote in the Swedish parliament in 1959, was vigorously resisted by the Swedish Employers' Confederation (SAF), whose spokesman attacked the scheme as an effort

to establish "absolute dominance over the Swedish capital market" (see Hadenius, 1965: 361; Molin, 1966: 45-58).

10. This fragmentation has been described in a growing body of literature that includes Fenno (1966), Horn (1970), Manley (1970), Pierce (1971), Schultze (1968), Sharkansky (1969), Wildavsky (1964).

11. See also Reagan (1961). Variations in the status of West European central banks are summarized in Kirschen et al., I (1964); U.S. Congress, House Committee on Banking and Currency (1970).

12. Especially pertinent in this connection is Steiner (1971). A brief but perceptive overview of the consequences of institutional fragmentation of public authority for economic policy is provided in Shonfield (1965: 298-357).

13. The standard source on the Fourth Republic in English is Williams (1954). For a subtle analysis of French political cleavages, see Hoffman (1963: 1-117).

14. For a survey of this period, see Rustow (1955: 90-115). An interesting study of the interaction of elites with parliamentary and bureaucratic power bases is provided by Lindeberg (1968).

15. The most recent general survey of Swedish politics is Hancock (1972); see also Board (1970).

16. The expression, "hegemonic party," is used by La Palombara and Weiner (1966: 35). On the Gaullists, see Charlot (1967).

17. What may be conceived as "economic power" and "political power," and the extent and ways that the former may be translatable into the latter are, of course, much debated. A cogent and concise discussion of the business corporation as a base of power for those who manage it is provided in Kaysen (1961). A recent collection presenting a wide range of views concerning the meanings and distribution of power in the United States is Gillam (1971). Without attempting to stake out a position among the contending viewpoints, it would seem that one can at least specify the kinds of resources at the disposal of specific people, which may enable them to exercise particular kinds of influence over others in specific situations. This is essentially the way Dahl (1970: 37-40, 86-92) looks at power.

18. The development of parties and interest groups suggests that any growth in a given group's organization that increases its ability to mobilize its resources in an arena of conflict puts pressure on other groups in the arena to achieve compensatory growth. For a discussion of British development that illustrates this kind of dynamic, see Beer (1965: 109-113. 255-261, 331-336). Such a dynamic is also clear in Swedish political development (Hadenius et al., 1969: 33-39). Of course, other factors may make a group unable to respond to the pressure of increasing organization by competing contenders for power. American business elites, however, do not seem to have been under such pressure, either in the labor market or the political arena, to anything like the extent to which British and Swedish business elites have been. These ideas are developed further in Part IV.

19. The question is certainly worth asking—and is asked—concerning countries with other types of political economy, including the Soviet Union.

20. Management in mature industrialism is discussed in Kerr et al. (1960: 133-164). For a fuller discussion of German management, see Hartmann (1959) and Shonfield (1965: 239-264).

21. A fascinating comparison of the sequence of development in Britain and Germany prior to the first world war is provided by Heidenheimer (1969).

22. On the German case, see Linz (1967 and Heidenheimer (1968: 41-87). On the Italian case, see Dogan (1967) and La Palombara (1966).

23. More precisely, the Wilson government tried to avoid both deflation and devaluation from October 1964, when it came into office, until July 1966, when it resorted to deflation in a continued effort to avoid devaluation, which it was finally forced to carry out in November 1967. By October 1966, total registered unemployment went over a half-million and remained above that level in all but one of the 44 months from then until Labor was voted out of office in June 1970. In percentage terms, unemployment averaged 2.4% in each of the three years from 1967 through 1969 and 2.6% in the first half of 1970. In only one of the thirteen years of Conservative government, from October 1951, to October 1964, did the annual average reach 2.5%. The average over the whole period from 1952 through 1964 was 1.6%, while the average over the whole period of Labor government from October 1964 through June 1970 was a little under 2.1%. Total registered unemployment and percentages, 1960-1967, from Department of Employment and Productivity, Statistics on Incomes, Prices, Employment & Production (various issues); 1968-April 1972, Department of Employment Gazette (May 1972); percentages, 1952-1959, Prest (1966: 246). Thus, during its last three-and-a-half years in office, the Wilson government permitted unemployment to remain at a substantially higher level than over the rest of the postwar period, even though that level was admittedly still low by American standards. The 2.6% average of registered unemployment in Britain in 1970 is estimated by the U.S. Bureau of Labor Statistics to be equivalent to 3.9% unemployment as measured in the United States (see U.S. Department of Labor, 1971: 352).

24. In January 1972, total registered unemployment reached 1,023,583 in the United Kingdom (including Northern Ireland), passing the million mark for the first time since the great Depression, except for the fuel crisis in February 1947. A coal strike raised the figure for February 1972, well above that, but in March, "by which time any lingering effects of the coal strike must have been small," unemployment was still 1,014,511 (Financial Times, 1972a, 1972b). The government's budget, announced shortly before the March unemployment figures were released, was aimed at bringing unemployment down through a large tax cut. However, this amounted to a reinforcement of a reversal in the trend that had already occurred. By May, total unemployment had fallen substantially below the million mark to a level of 901,592 (Financial Times, 1972c, 1972a). In Great Britain (i.e., excluding Northern Ireland), unemployment was 4.3% in January and March, 4.2% in April, and 3.8% in May.

25. According to the Labor Party's weekly newspaper, a new book by the group of Conservative MPs referred to argues that the lowest level of unemployment that it was now reasonable to aim at was 600,000 (Labour Weekly, 1972). This corresponds to about 2.6% or, as the newspaper fails to point out, the average during the previous Labor government's last half-year in office.

26. On the German case, see W. S. Woytinsky's autobiography (1961: 458-472). As director of research and statistics of the German Federation of Free Trade Unions—the ADGB, which was associated with the Social Democratic Party—Woytinsky won the Federation leadership's backing for a program of deficit financed public works but failed to overcome the Social Democratic Party's resistance to the idea, led by Rudolph Hilferding, the economic theorist and former Minister of Finance, who condemned the idea as anti-Marxist. On the British case, see the biography of Ernest Bevin by Bullock (1960: I, chaps. 16-18). Bevin, much influenced by his experience of serving with John Maynard Keynes on the Macmillan Committee, led the TUC's opposition to the deflationary policy that MacDonald and Snowden insisted upon.

27. It is hard to believe that a break with orthodoxy would not have made a difference. While Chancellor Heinrich Brüning doggedly pursued a policy of budget balancing, unemployment in Germany rose from 1,320,000 in September 1929 (half a year before Brüning took office) to a peak of over six million in early 1932 (just prior to Brüning's dismissal), and electoral support for the Nazis mushroomed from 810,000 in the 1928 Reichstag election to a peak of 13,745,000 in the July, 1932 Reichstag election (Bullock, 1964: 144, 152, 217, 230).

28. On the relationships between the German army and unions during the first world war, see Feldman (1966). On Schleicher's abortive efforts to mobilize a coalition around a reflationary program at the end of 1932, see Bullock (1964: 238-48).

29. The Swedish Social Democrats' innovation in economic policy is described in Landgren (1960: 9-99). Ernst Wigforss, the prime mover in the break with orthodoxy, provides an account in his memoirs (1954: 17-41). The ideological implications of the episode are discussed by Lewin (1967: 7-117). The political realignment that the policy innovation made possible and on which its implementation depended is described by Nyman (1944).

30. The case for the proposition cannot be argued here. It seems obvious as far as the MacDonald government is concerned. Even if the Wilson government did not precipitate a similar break with the unions, its imposition of a wage freeze, increase in unemployment, and abortive effort to reform industrial relations by statute were certainly not calculated to arouse enthusiastic support of its organized labor constituency. Perhaps the Attlee government can also be said to have failed to make the most of its political resources, at least when it called an election in 1951 at what was probably the worst possible moment.

31. See also Bailey (1964: 129-149).

32. President Johnson's orientation to the business community is discussed in an interesting article by Gass (1965).

REFERENCES

AARON, H. (1967) "Social Security: international comparisons," pp. 13-48 in O. Eckstein (ed.) Studies in the Economics of Income Maintenance. Washington, D.C.: Brookings Institution.

ABEL-SMITH, B. and P. TOWNSEND (1965) The Poor and the Poorest. London: G. Bell.

ALEXANDER, S. S. (1948) "Opposition to deficit spending for the prevention of unemployment," pp. 177-198 in Income, Employment and Public Policy. New York: W. W. Norton.

ARNDT, H. W. (1944) The Economic Lessons of the Nineteen-Thirties. London: Oxford Univ. Press.

BAILEY, S. K. (1964) Congress Makes a Law. New York: Vintage.

BEER, S. H. (1965) British Politics in the Collectivist Age. New York: Alfred A. Knopf.

BEVERIDGE, W. H. (1944) Full Employment in a Free Society. London: George Allen & Unwin.

BIEMILLER, A. J. (1964) Labor Looks at the 88th Congress. Washington, D.C.: American Federation of Labor and Congress of Industrial Organizations.

BOARD, J. B., Jr. (1970) The Government and Politics of Sweden. Boston: Houghton Mifflin.

BRITTAN, S. (1970) Steering the Economy. Harmondsworth: Penguin.

BULLOCK, A. (1964) Hitler, A Study in Tyranny. Rev. ed. New York: Harper & Row.

――― (1960) The LIfe and Times of Ernest Bevin, I. London: Heinemann.

BURNHAM, W. D. (1971) Communication. Amer. Pol. Sci. Rev. LXV (December): 1149-1152.

――― (1970) Critical Elections and the Mainsprings of American Politics. New York: W. W. Norton.

――― (1967) "Party systems and the political process," pp. 277-307 in W. N. Chambers and W. D. Burnham (eds.) The American Party Systems: Stages of Political Development. New York: Oxford Univ. Press.

――― (1965) "The changing shape of the American political universe," Amer. Pol. Sci. Rev. LIX (March): 7-28.

BUTLER, D. E. and A. KING (1966) The British General Election of 1966. London: Macmillan.

CAIRE, G. (1971) Les syndicats ouvriers. Paris: Presses Universitaires de France.

CAVES, R. E. et al. (1968) Britain's Economic Prospects. Washington, D.C.: Brookings Institution.

CHARLOT, J. (1967) L'UNR: étude du pouvoir au sein d'un parti politique. Paris: Armand Colin.

CLEGG, H. A. and R. ADAMS (1957) The Employers' Challenge: A Study of the National Shipbuilding and Engineering Disputes of 1957. Oxford: Basil Blackwell.

CROSLAND, C.A.R. (1956) The Future of Socialism. London: Jonathan Cape.

DAHL, R. A. (1970) Modern Political Analysis. Englewood Cliffs: Prentice-Hall.

――― [ed.] (1966) Political Oppositions in Western Democracies. New Haven: Yale Univ. Press.

Department of Employment Gazette (May, 1972). London: HMSO.

Department of Employment and Productivity (1968-April 1972) Statistics on Incomes, Prices, Employment and Production. London: HMSO.

DOGAN, M. (1967) "Political cleavage and social stratification in France and Italy," pp. 129-165 in S. M. Lipset and S. Rokkan (eds.) Party Systems and Voter Alignments. New York: Free Press.

Economic Report of the President (1971). Washington, D.C.: Government Printing Office.

EDELMAN, M. and R. W. FLEMING (1965) The Politics of Wage-Price Decisions. Urbana: Univ. of Illinois Press.

EHRMANN, H. W. (1968) Politics in France. Boston: Little, Brown.

EPSTEIN, L. D. (1967) Political Parties in Western Democracies. New York: Frederick A. Praeger.

FELDMAN, G. D. (1966) Army, Industry and Labor in Germany, 1914-1918. Princeton: Princeton Univ. Press.

FENNO, R. F., Jr. (1966) The Power of the Purse: Appropriations Politics in Congress. Boston: Little, Brown.

Financial Times (1972a) London: January 21.

――― (1972b) London: March 24.

––– (1972c) London: March 22.

––– (1972d) London: May 19.

GARVIN, J. L. (1932-1969) The Life of Joseph Chamberlain, I. London: Macmillan.

GASS, O. (1965) "The political economy of the great society," Commentary (October): 31-36.

GILLAM, R. [ed.] (1971) Power in Postwar America. Boston: Little, Brown.

GORDON, R. A. (1967) The Goal of Full Employment. New York: John Wiley.

GREENSTONE, J. D. (1969) Labor in American Politics. New York: Alfred A. Knopf.

HADENIUS, S. (1965) "Partiers beslutsprocess och tjanstepensionsfrågan," Statsvetenskaplig Tidskrift 68: 343-364.

––– H. WIESLANDER, and B. MOLIN (1969) Sverige efter 1900: En modern politisk historia. Sockholm: Bokförlaget Aldus/Bonniers.

HANCOCK, H. D. (1972) Sweden: The Politics of Postindustrial Change. Hinsdale, Ill.: Dryden.

HARTMANN, H. (1959) Authority and Organization in German Management. Princeton: Princeton Univ. Press.

HAYWARD, J.E.S. (1966) "Interest groups and incomes policy in France." British J. of Industrial Relations IV (July): 165-200.

HEATH, J. (1969) John F. Kennedy and the Business Community. Chicago: Univ. of Chicago Press.

HEIDENHEIMER, A. J. (1969) "Trade unions, benefit systems, and party mobilization styles: 'horizontal' influences on the British Labour and German Social Democratic Parties." Comparative Politics 1 (April): 313-342.

––– and F. C. LANGDON (1968) Business Associations and the Financing of Political Parties. The Hague: Martinus Nijhoff.

HELLER, W. W. (1967) New Dimensions of Political Economy. New York: W. W. Norton.

HENIG, S. and J. PINDER [eds.] (1969) European Political Parties. London: George Allen & Unwin.

HOFFMANN, S. (1963) "Paradoxes of the French political community," pp. 1-117 in S. Hoffmann et al. In Search of France. Cambridge: Harvard Univ. Press.

HOLBORN, H. (1969) A History of Modern Germany, 1840-1945. New York: Alfred A. Knopf.

HORN, S. (1970) Unused Power. Washington, D.C.: Brookings Institution.

HUNTINGTON, S. P. (1968) Political Order in Changing Societies. New Haven: Yale Univ. Press.

KASSALOW, E. M. (1969) Trade Unions and Industrial Relations: An International Comparison. New York: Random House.

KAYSEN, C. (1961) "The corporation: how much power? what scope?" pp. 85-105 in E. S. Mason (ed.) The Corporation in Modern Society. Cambridge: Harvard Univ. Press.

KERR, C., J. T. DUNLOP, F. H. HARBISON, and C. A. MYERS (1960) Industrialism and Industrial Man. Cambridge: Harvard Univ. Press.

KIRSCHEN, E. S. et al. (1964) Economic Policy in Our Time, I. Amsterdam: North Holland Publishing.

Labour Weekly (1972) 12. London: June 9: 12.

LANDGREN, K.-G. (1960) Den "nya ekomien" i Sverige. Stockholm: Almqvist & Wiksell.

LA PALOMBARA, J. (1966) Interest Groups in Italian Politics. Princeton: Princeton Univ. Press.

————— and M. WEINER [eds.] (1966) Political Parties and Political Development. Princeton: Princeton Univ. Press.

LEUCHTENBURG, W. E. (1963) Franklin D. Roosevelt and the New Deal, 1932-1940. New York: Harper & Row.

LEWIN, L. (1967) Planhushållnings debatten. Stockholm: Almqvist & Wiksell.

LINDBECK, A. (1968) Svensk ekonomisk politik. Stockholm: Bokförlaget Aldus/ Bonniers.

LINDEBERG, S. O. (1968) Nödhjälp och samhällsneutralitet: Svensk arbet-slöshetspolitik, 1920-1923. Lund: Uniskol/Bokförlaget Universitet ock skola.

LINZ, J. J. (1967) "Cleavage and consensus in West German politics: the early fifties," pp. 283-321 in S. M. Lipset and S. Rokkan (eds.) Party Systems and Voter Alignments. New York: Free Press.

LIPSET, S. M. and S. ROKKAN (1967) "Cleavage structures, party systems, and voter alignments: an introduction," pp. 1-64 in S. M. Lipset and S. Rokkan (eds.) Party Systems and Voter Alignments. New York: Free Press.

LUNDBERG, E. (1957) Business Cycles and Economic Policy (trans. J. Potter). Cambridge: Harvard Univ. Press.

MADDISON, A. (1964) Economic Growth in the West. New York: Twentieth Century Fund.

MANLEY, J. F. (1970) The Politics of Finance: The House Committee on Ways and Means. Boston: Little, Brown.

MOLIN, B. (1966) "Swedish party politics: a case study," Scandinavian Pol. Studies I: 45-58.

NEUSTADT, R. E. (1960) Presidential Power: The Politics of Leadership. New York: John Wiley.

New York Times (1972): May 31.

NYMAN, O. (1944) Krisuppgörelsen mellan socialdemokraterna och bonde-förbundet. Uppsala: Almqvist & Wiksell.

Organization for Economic Co-operation and Development (1970) National Accounts of OECD Countries. Paris: OECD.

PECHMAN, J. A., H. A. AARON, and M. K. TAUSSIG (1968) Social Security: Perspectives for Reform. Washington, D.C.: Brookings Institution.

PELLING, H. (1963) A History of British Trade Unionism. Baltimore: Penguin.

PIERCE, L.C. (1971) The Politics of Fiscal Policy Formation. Pacific Palisades: Goodyear Publishing.

PREST, A. R. [ed.] (1966) The UK Economy. London: Weidenfeld & Nicholson.

REAGAN, M. D. (1961) "The political structure of the federal reserve system." Amer. Pol. Sci. Rev. LV (March): 64-76.

ROHL, J.C.G. (1967) Germany Without Bismarck: The Crisis of Government in the Second Reich, 1890-1900. Berkeley: Univ. of California Press.

RUSTOW, D. A. (1955) The Politics of Compromise. Princeton: Princeton Univ. Press.

SCHOENBAUM, D. (1967) Hitler's Social Revolution. New York: Anchor.

SCHORR, A. L. (1972) "The duplex society." New York Times (June 4).

SCHULTZE, C. L. (1968) The Politics and Economics of Public Spending. Washington, D.C.: Brookings Institution.

SELLIER, F. (1970) Dynamique des besoins sociaux. Paris: Les Editions Ouvrières.

SHARKANSKY, I. (1969) The Politics of Taxing and Spending. Indianapolis: Bobbs-Merrill.

SHONFIELD, A. (1965) Modern Capitalism: The Changing Balance of Public and Private Power. New York: Oxford Univ. Press.

SKIDELSKY, R. (1967) Politicians and the Slump. London: Macmillan.

SMITH, D. C. (1966) Incomes Policies: Some Foreign Experiences and Their Relevance for Canada. Ottawa: Queen's Printer.

Social Insurance and Allied Services (1942) London: HMSO.

SORRENTINO, C. (1970) "Unemployment in the United States and seven foreign countries." Monthly Labor Rev. 93 (September): 12-23.

Statistisk årsbok (1970) Stockholm: Statistiska Centralbryån.

––– (1968) Stockholm: Statistika Centralbyrån.

––– (1964) Stockholm: Statistika Centralbyrån.

STEIN, H. (1969) The Fiscal Revolution in America. Chicago: Univ. of Chicago Press.

STEINER, G. Y. (1971) The State of Welfare. Washington, D.C.: Brookings Institution.

SUNDQUIST, J. L. (1968) Politics and Policy: The Eisenhower, Kennedy and Johnson Years. Washington, D.C.: Brookings Institution.

Svenska folkets inkomster (1970). Statens offentliga utredningar 34. Stockholm.

The Swedish Budget (1970) Stockholm: Ministry of Finance.

––– (1969) Stockholm: Ministry of Finance.

The Swedish Economy (1972) Stockholm: Ministry of Finance and National Institute of Economic Research.

––– (1971) Stockholm: Ministry of Finance and National Institute of Economic Research.

TITMUSS, R. M. (1960) The Irresponsible Society. London: Fabian Society.

––– (1958) Essays on 'The Welfare State.' London: George Allen & Unwin.

UHR, C. G. (1966) Sweden's Social Security System. Washington, D.C.: Government Printing Office.

ULMAN, L. and R. J. FLANAGAN (1971) Wage Restraint: A Study of Incomes Policies in Western Europe. Berkeley: Univ. of California Press.

U.S. Bureau of the Census (1971, 1970) Statistical Abstract of the United States, 1971 and 1970. Washington, D.C.: Government Printing Office.

U.S. Congress, House, Committee on Banking and Currency (1970) Activities by Various Central Banks to Promote Economic and Social Programs. 91st Congress, 2nd Session.

U.S. Department of Labor (1971) Handbook of Labor Statistics 1971. Washington, D.C.: Government Printing Office.

WAXMAN, C. I. [ed.] (1968) The End of Ideology Debate. New York: Simon & Schuster.

WESTERLIND, E. and R. BECKMAN (1965) Sweden's Economy. Stockholm: Bokförlaget Prisma.

WIGFORSS, E. (1954) Minnen. Stockholm: Tidens Förlag.

WILDAVSKY, A. (1964) The Politics of the Budgetary Process. Boston: Little, Brown.

WILLIAMS, P. (1954) Politics in Postwar France. London: Longmans, Green.

WOYTINSKY, W. S. (1961) Stormy Passage. New York: Vanguard.

ANDREW MARTIN wrote this paper while he was a Research Fellow at the Harvard University West European Studies Program and Center for International Affairs. He received his Ph.D. at Columbia University; and he has taught at Columbia and at the University of Massachusetts, Amherst. He is currently Assistant Professor of Political Science at Boston University.

EDITORS' INTRODUCTION TO THE SERIES

This series of papers in comparative politics serves several purposes. It offers an additional and regular outlet for publishing the research products of a rapidly growing and intrinsically large and variegated field. It also provides an alternative to the only two kinds of outlets now available: journal publication of rather short pieces (about the length of which harassed editors have become increasingly restrictive) and book publication of extensive work. The series was, in fact, originally conceived chiefly for that purpose, it being unlikely that all good work in the field could be condensed, without serious loss, to the level of a normal journal article or would reach, without padding, the length of a normal book.

The series also has two economic advantages. Present subscribers to political science journals are often forced to buy many articles in which they have no interest for the sake of obtaining those of genuine importance to them; journals thus intrinsically entail higher costs to the consumer than series of individually available papers—or else the consumer lives, via free reprints, off the charity of publishers and authors. Moreover, if the papers are offered as a series, as well as being individually available, publishers can more readily overlook some unavoidable, but intellectually dubious, considerations of their own: for example, the size of a work's potential market (not actual merit) or the prevalent economic biases against provisional reports on continuing work, which often are as interesting and instructive as the finished products, and as important to the development of the field.

Our conception of comparative politics is not a narrow one. For that reason, quite apart from the distinction of authorship, we are especially pleased that the monograph by Namenwirth and Lasswell* should have inaugurated this series. It illustrates two important aspects of editorial policy. We cannot conceive of any intellectually tenable reason for regarding comparative politics as the study of foreign governments only and excluding American studies from its scope. We also cannot see why useful comparisons should not be made between different segments of a polity or, as in this case, between conditions in the nominally same case at different points in time. Weighty reasons could in fact be given for considering such comparisons especially worth making.

Comparative politics normally is, but need not be, cross-national or cross-cultural in the literal sense. While admitting a bias in favor of wide-ranging studies, we consider eligible for the series any study, including case studies and purely abstract papers, that clearly share the overall aim of comparative political studies and make some progress toward achieving it: the formulation of valid theoretical generalizations about the structures, behavior, and performance of polities.

—Harry Eckstein and Ted Robert Gurr

---

*"The Changing Language of American Values: A Computer Study of Selected Party Platforms," by J. Zvi Namenwirth and Harold D. Lasswell. *Sage Professional Papers in Comparative Politics 01-001.* Beverly Hills: Sage Publications, 1970. 72 pages.

ABOUT THIS SERIES

Ordering Information

As separates:

Papers may be purchased separately (most are priced between $2.00 and $3.00 each). Orders totaling less than $10.00 must be accompanied by payment. If you wish to receive announcements about forthcoming titles in the Sage Professional Papers series, please send your name and address to:

SAGE PROFESSIONAL PAPERS IN COMPARATIVE POLITICS
Sage Publications, Inc.
275 South Beverly Drive
Beverly Hills, California 90212

On subscription:

Annual subscriptions to twelve papers are available. (Subscriptions should be entered on a calendar year basis.) Subscription prices, for unbound sets of papers (mailed four at a time, three times each year), are:

	One Year	Two Years	Three Years
Institutions	$21.00	$41.00	$60.00
Individuals*	$12.00	$23.00	$33.00

To expedite service, individual orders must be prepaid.

Clothbound volumes:

The bound library edition is available in three clothbound parts (each part containing four papers) per volume. Bound parts will be published approximately 30 days after publication of separate paper editions. *Subscription price:* $10.00 per part ($30.00 per year), if subscription is entered during year of publication, only. *Regular price:* if bound parts are ordered separately, or after publication, the cost will be $12.50 per part ($37.50 for a complete annual volume).

ORDER FROM

SAGE PUBLICATIONS, INC.
275 South Beverly Drive
Beverly Hills, California 90212

SAGE PUBLICATIONS LTD
St George's House / 44 Hatton Garden
London EC1N 8ER

For complete list of titles available in this series please see opposite page

SAGE PROFESSIONAL PAPERS IN COMPARATIVE POLITICS

VOLUME 1 (1970)

(Continued)

VOLUME 3 (1972)

VOLUME 4 (1973)

SAGE PUBLICATIONS, INC.
275 S. Beverly Dr. / Beverly Hills, CA. 90212

SAGE PUBLICATIONS LTD
44 Hatton Garden, London EC1N 8E

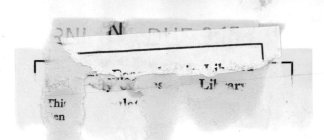